The Semi-Transparent Envelope

Sue Roe,
Susan Sellers,
Nicole Ward Jouve
with Michèle Roberts

The Semi-Transparent Envelope

Women Writing — Feminism and Fiction

Marion Boyars
London • New York

First published in Great Britain and the United States in 1994
by Marion Boyars Publishers
24 Lacy Road, London SW15 1NL
237 East 39th Street, New York, NY 10016

Distributed in Australia and New Zealand by Peribo Pty Ltd, Terrey Hills, NSW

British Library Cataloguing in Publication Data

Roe, Sue et al
   Semi-Transparent Envelope: Women Writing
   — Feminism and Fiction
   I. Title
   809.3

Library of Congress Cataloging in Publication Data

Roe, Sue et al
     The semi-transparent envelope : Women writing—feminism and
fiction / Sue Roe, Susan Sellers, Nicole Ward Jouve, with Michèle
Roberts.
     Contents: Shelving the self / Sue Roe — Writing new fictions /
Susan Sellers — The red road / Nicole Ward Jouve — Where now,
where next? / Roe, Sellers, Ward Jouve — Post-script/Michèle Roberts.
     1. English fiction—Women authors—History and criticism—Theory,
etc.   2. Feminism and literature—England—History—20th century.
3. Women and literature—England—History—20th century.
4. Authorship—Sex differences. I. Sellers, Susan. II. Ward
Jouve, Nicole. III. Title
PR888.F45R64   1994
823.009'9287—dc20

ISBN 0–7145–2967–2 Original Paperback

Typeset by Ann Buchan (Typesetters)
Printed by Itchen Printers Ltd.

Contents

Previous publications by the same authors

Sue Roe
Estella: Her Expectations (fiction), Harvester, reissued 1987.
Women Reading Women's Writing (criticism), Harvester, 1987.
Writing and Gender: Virginia Woolf's Writing Practice (criticism), Harvester, 1990.
Virginia Woolf's *Jacob's Room* (ed.), Penguin Modern Classics Edition, 1992.
Short stories and poems in various anthologies.

Susan Sellers
Writing Differences (criticism), Open University and St Martin's, 1988.
Delighting the Heart: A Notebook by Women Writers (creative writing handbook), The Women's Press, 1989, reissued 1994.
'Coming to Writing' and Other Essays (translation), Harvard, 1991.
Feminist Criticism, Harvester and Toronto, 1991.
Language and Sexual Difference (literary theory), Macmillan and St Martin's, 1991.
Taking Reality by Surprise: Writing for Pleasure and Publication (creative writing handbook), The Women's Press, 1991, reissued 1994.
Three Steps on the Ladder of Writing (translation), Columbia, 1993.
The Hélène Cixous Reader, Routledge, 1994.

Nicole Ward Jouve
Le Spectre du gris (fiction), des femmes, 1977.
Baudelaire: A Fire to Conquer Darkness (criticism), Macmillan, 1980.
L'Entremise (fiction), des femmes, 1980.
Shades of Grey (fiction), Virago, 1981.
'The Streetcleaner': The Yorkshire Ripper Case on Trial (criticism), Marion Boyars, 1986.
Colette (criticism), Harvester and Indiana, 1987.

White Woman Speaks with Forked Tongue: Criticism as Autobiography, Routledge, 1991.
Un Homme nommé Zapolski (criticism), des femmes, 1983.

Michèle Roberts

A Piece of the Night (fiction), The Women's Press, 1978.
Tales I tell My Mother (fiction, with Zoë Fairbairns, Sara Maitland, Valerie Miner and Michelene Wandor), Journeyman Press, 1978.
Touch Papers (poetry, with Judith Kazantzis and Michelene Wandor), Allison and Busby, 1982.
The Visitation (fiction), The Women's Press, 1983.
The Wild Girl (fiction), Methuen, 1984.
The Mirror of the Mother (poetry), Methuen, 1986.
The Book of Mrs Noah (fiction), Methuen, 1987.
More Tales I tell My Mother (fiction), Journeyman Press, 1987.
In the Red Kitchen (fiction), Methuen, 1990.
Psyche and the Hurricane (poetry), Methuen, 1991.
Daughters of the House (fiction), Virago, 1992.
During Mother's Absence (fiction), Virago, 1993.

Life is not a series of gig lamps symmetrically arranged;
but a luminous halo, a semi-transparent envelope
surrounding us from the beginning of consciousness
to the end.

Virginia Woolf, 'Modern Fiction'

Introduction

This book is about four women's writing. It offers insights into the processes, which for women, inscribe the making of a work of art, and glimpses, from different angles, into the evolution of a work of fiction. We have written it because the procedure of artistic production continues to fascinate us and because we wanted to investigate whether the act of artistic engagement might mean special things for women.

One of the ways in which feminism has highlighted the sexuality of writing is by focusing on the connections between writing and the body. We had each become interested, from our different perspectives and in our different ways, in the challenge posed by writing about the body; in deciding to compare our thoughts on this issue we found that there was much we had all discovered, in the process of sketching out our ideas, about the business of describing and inscribing femininity. We found that we were all asking questions about personal and cultural identity, sexual identity, activity and passivity, subjugation and authority, gender and writing, biography and autobiography, passion, transgression, romanticism and pornography, privacy and performance, revelation and disguise. Some questions seem to come up repeatedly for all of us in the course of our writing practices. What is the relation between writing and desire? Between writing and pleasure? Is that pleasure sexed? Can we cross the sexual divide, and does the imaginary aspect of writing mean that we necessarily do so? What difference has twenty years of feminism made for the ways in which today's women writers think about their craft? Not all of these questions are specifically feminine or feminist of course: they are aspects of any writer's struggle with the process of creation. What components, then, of that inextricable engagement writers enter into as they struggle with the compulsive, elusive, often intangible object of their art are specific to the woman writer?

In opening our sketchbooks to the reader, and in using material published here for the first time to demonstrate our discoveries about our craft, we hope not only to share some of our insights into the ways in which writing practice works, but also to reveal the extent to which, throughout much of the creative process, we are often working in the dark. Writing is not only about pleasure and desire, it is also about fear. About the unexpected. The unwanted. The not-yet-known.

By taking our readers — as it were — inside our studios, by opening our sketchbooks and offering glimpses into the evolution of our work as it unfolds, we aim to present a multi-layered agenda. As critics — particularly as feminist critics — we have each developed our own reading practice. We have each negotiated a route through the proliferation of theories, models and positions available to the reader which we apply, here, to our own writing process. Yet writing entails a different starting point and mode of procedure to the task of literary criticism. As we write we undergo a process of struggle and change. We are brought to ask fundamental questions about ourselves and the world, questions which our writing poses, complicates, challenges and, sometimes, resolves. Thus we are concerned here not only to analyze writing practices and to theorize the woman writer's agenda. Writing creates rather than reflects agendas. It stretches us, alters us, prompting us to revision, reconsider, reconstruct. This book endeavours to tell the story of that process.

In 'Shelving the Self', Sue Roe explores the difficulties and complexities involved in developing a character who seems determined to sabotage her relationship with her creator. In the course of the author's journey back into the novel a new fiction begins to emerge. While the character of the original novel fights to avoid suffocation, the new heroine vies for space. As the story of this struggle unfolds, Sue Roe describes her experience of drawing from life as a way of finding a new route out of, then back into, her own medium. The desirous, sometimes passionate, often terrifying engagement with language is obsessional, emotional and erotic. As Sue Roe compares the respective demands of writing and drawing, she encounters the model as well as the muse. Both are encounters rarely discussed from the viewpoint of the woman writer. In 'Shelving the Self' they are explored in detail. The stages through which a woman writer moves in her struggle with her art entails the adoption of many different and warring personae; she is victim, murderer, lover, voyeur, artist, model, other. The struggle is also a struggle with herself.

Fiction can be likened to a magnet, attracting, drawing to the surface and shaping a wealth of impressions, questions, convictions. Some of the sources are conscious, others are not. Yet the completed text can appear both rootless and seamless. While each work of art has its own gestation and life-story, there are nevertheless a number of elements that recur in the writing of fiction. In 'Writing New Fictions' Susan Sellers explores these elements through the process of writing one novel, discussing such aspects of literary composition as imagery, theme, characterization, story-line and form.

Some of these components have specific implications for the woman writer. As Susan Sellers' protagonist sets out on a quest for self-identity the dilemmas she faces are echoed by dilemmas in the writing. Where are the models for such a quest? How might it be possible to embody this journey with such traditional fictional pleasures as drama, intrigue and suspense? How can the culturally conditioned dream world of fantasy and romance be portrayed in novel form? Is such a world a valid subject for fiction? Or does its internal focus automatically render it less important than novels that deal with 'real' events? Is the purpose of fiction to explain and so confirm us in our relation to the world? Or can it play a more transgressive role?

The starting point for Nicole Ward Jouve's 'The Red Road' is the revisioning of literary legend and mythic writing. She asks what would have happened if adolescent Rimbaud had met with child Colette? Detailing how and why the idea of such an encounter occurred to her, she includes extracts from the novella the idea produced. Her text re-imagines the 'real'

Rimbaud and Colette as they are known, or imagined, through
their biographies, but also reinvents them on the basis of their
own writing, their own self-inventions. She considers tradition, contemporary (female?) talent, and explores the so-
called relationship between content and form. She reflects on
the rules for writing and asks: are there any left today? Above
all, her concern is with gender and writing. How does a
woman writer imagine a male character of such fierce rebel-
liousness as Rimbaud and who was such a woman-hater? Can
she imagine the route he would have had to follow to find a
way out of that hate? And to this end can she use, or must she
reforge, Colette's ingenious forgeries of childhood and motherhood?

The muse is always tantalizing, always elusive, but for the
writer so is the model. We sketch out our characters in the
presence of our predecessors. Our influences are crucial,
though not always conscious. The work of other women
artists inspires us, as does the work of male painters and
writers. We may want to implicitly pay tribute to, or harbour
a secret wish to kill off, our ghosts. Our materials, as writers,
are limitless, though they impose their own constraints. Language may be plied until it becomes tactile, but it does not
soften like charcoal or harden like paint. As critics, we may
analyze our own and one another's achievements; as practi-
tioners we can never say whether the risk pays off. We look,
we tell, we wait. We will always do it differently next time.
The kind of courage it requires is something never easy to
explain.

Suspense was to be of the essence.Thus we chose to proceed from complete to partial tease. In Jamesian fashion Sue
Roe writes about a novel we never see, which in the process
of being finished generates another novel, which we never see
either. She explores the muse and model, her inspiration for
the two works. Susan Sellers unbinds a novel in an endeavour
to work her way back through the writing process. In telling
this story, she offers us fragments of the original, the illustra-
tive, rebound leaves of a new account. Nicole Ward Jouve
does present substantial extracts from her novella. The fiction

is there in part. But the ending, which is the crux, is missing. The reader is left to imagine it, on the basis of what has been suggested. Here the reader is invited to become the writer: placed in the position of inventing, of teasing out, if she or he will, if the lure has been enough. Of travelling, in turn, the red road.

As a work of art evolves, the self is engaged in a series of challenges: to disappear, to collude, to cheat, to master, to hold back, to reveal, to look. To see, to look and to tell become not only challenges but quests. The struggle begins to be a matter of life and death. In describing our struggles, we necessarily also reveal some of our strategies for survival.

Painters may choose to exhibit their sketches alongside their other work. For a writer, only the completed work can offer anything approaching a whole response. In offering our sketches for display we cannot, of course, tell the entire story. What we aim to present in this book is as full, as comprehensive and as vivid a picture as we can of some of the events which take place as our respective struggles unfold. By offering — as it were — to exhibit our sketches, we hope we may have found ways of telling new stories about _how_, as women writers, our writing is important to us as we work to understand and communicate the world as it appears to us today.

Where Now, Where Next?

The following conversation between
Nicole Ward Jouve, Susan Sellers and Sue Roe
was recorded on 12 December, 1992.

SUSAN: Perhaps a good place to begin would be with the title: *The Semi-Transparent Envelope*. Sue, this title was initially your suggestion and perhaps you could say what prompted you to think of it?

SUE: It comes from Virginia Woolf's Essay 'Modern Fiction' in which she is arguing against the constructions of people like Arnold Bennett, Wells and Galsworthy who were using their fiction as copies of 'life'. She wanted to get at something much more flexible, much more permeable: she wanted to think in terms of the novel's being an original rather than a copy. The quotation is 'Life is not a series of gig lamps symmetrically arranged; but a luminous halo, a semi-transparent envelope surrounding us from the beginning of consciousness to the end.' This links up with her work on Dorothy Richardson where she identifies Dorothy Richardson's language as flexible, elastic, and what it raises is the question of whether women can use language in more flexible ways than men.

SUSAN: For me the 'semi-transparent envelope' relates to the central image — which I also in turn use as a title — for the work I discuss here: the aquarium as a container, as a place through which to perceive and make sense of the world.

NICOLE: What the envelope brought to me is thoughts about the placenta, the womb. I wondered whether a woman writer would have a different relationship to the idea of the mother and the womb from a man writer. We do, after all, all come from the same place, but women have a womb, are at least potentially 'envelopes', so is the relationship the same? Certainly my piece on Rimbaud is full of a search for home, for a house, an attic, cellars and then, eventually, the empty inn, and there is this sense of searching for some kind of envelope that would do — and what does it do to you if you find it. . . ? And then, do you put a letter in the envelope? Is it blank? Claudine Hermann in *Les Voleuses de Langue* argues that culturally women have been seen as blank letters or blank envelopes that men send each other — you wonder what's in the letter? There are hundreds of paintings (Dutch and other) of women receiving, reading, sending letters. Also Virginia Woolf doesn't say whether the envelope is life as we see it, or as it contains us. If consciousness is the envelope: does it wrap around us, and does it wrap around the world? When one is writing, is one trying to see through into the world or is one trying to create the semi-transparent envelope so that the circulation between self and the world is established, or re-established? And if the envelope is semi-transparent, how fragile. For me there is the idea of elasticity but also fragility in that metaphor, and I think it may be appropriate to our pieces since in all of them there is a precariousness in the search for home, whatever home may mean.

SUSAN: I think that it also raises questions about what fiction is, about what it is we ask fiction to do. For me the 'semi-transparent envelope' also evokes both the difficulties of trying to see more clearly, and the necessity of attempting to do so: of struggling towards a less opaque vision, towards greater comprehension. And I think the value of fiction as opposed to other forms of discourse in this regard is suggested by the notion of 'envelope', which for me relates to the form of fiction, to the particular way fiction gives us reality, or perceptions of reality, and invites us to participate in its experience through identification, empathy and so on — thereby providing us with more 'transparent' insights into the nature of that experience, that world, and hence, by extension, our own.

NICOLE: What you say reminds me of Paul Ricoeur, whom I was reading recently, talking about literature. One of the functions of literature, he says, is to make us feel at home with the world. It creates that impossible home for the time that we read, and that is why we read. It is not just a question of making sense, but of making the world a habitable place. In terms of women writing — and without

wanting to generalize — it makes me think that quite a few
women writers take on the double burden of writing to
make a home of the world, to make it habitable, while still
pursuing a traditional function of mothering, of being the
home creator: so that you double up when you write. And
in a funny way I think your body doubles up as well: that
somehow there is a kind of caring that goes into the
writing, a kind of care for the reader that entails using the
body and its relation to the world in a particular way. I am
thinking especially of Michèle Roberts' _In the Red Kitchen_,
in which there is so much stuff about the home; it is
haunted by past presences. There is a relationship to the
inner skin of the house, its walls, its basement, its food,
that acts as a metaphor for the novel's form. That is
specifically woman-centred for me.

SUE: I get worried about the amount of housekeeping the
house of fiction seems to demand, and about the problem of
splitting yourself in the way you need to because you have to
be wholly yourself both to housekeep in real life, as it were,
and to do the housekeeping in your fiction. How deeply
demanding that is of your integrity, and yet it is only one
aspect of life and only one responsibility among many. I also
want to find some way of thinking about what kind of
integrity it actually is that the house of fiction requires of you,
because once it requires your profoundest integrity how then
do you get the necessary distance from it? Enough to be the
author, with authority and control over the thing you are
making. I get very anxious about that confusion, about the
implicit autobiographical element: about how much of the
self you want to give, how much of the self you want to shelve,
and how much of the self you are capable of shelving. And
I wonder whether this is a problem that male writers encounter, this notion of total biological or perhaps bodily integrity
that your text seems to demand of you; and what do you do
about the fact that it seems to leave nothing of yourself over,
and yet you don't want to write about yourself? I keep coming
back to Virginia Woolf in _A Room of One's Own_ saying she

wants to 'use writing as an art, not as a method of self-expression'.

NICOLE: This idea of self-exposure, wanting to avoid the autobiographical, wanting to avoid talking about yourself, reminds me of a practice of a number of contemporary women writers who deliberately show in order to conceal and who know how to make a show, an act, of their supposed selves and their supposed lives in order to conceal their real selves and their real lives. In a sense this is the reverse of what I was saying earlier, but I think it may be there in anybody who writes. I am thinking of writers like Marie Cardinal whom I heard say 'if you like, and you may not like because I am sixty and I'm fat, I will show you my arse, but I will never ever tell you how I use it'. It is exposing what you don't mind showing in order to conceal what is really important, call it integrity or self. I was also thinking of the way Angela Carter talks about Colette saying 'Look, but don't touch' or 'You may look as long as you pay'. You're paying for the spectacle she is willing to produce, not *her*. Colette earned money from selling stories about her life and this enabled her to conceal and keep private what she wanted to keep private. Colette writes endlessly about this, about the decency and secrecy that are preserved by display.

SUE: But I do think there is a problem here. You talked earlier about the caretaking of the reader that the woman writer tends to do, and I do think there is a different expectation when reading women's writing. There is an assumption that revelation is deeply autobiographical and that what the reader is reading is the deeply revealed, exposed self. As you say, the treatment of the self doesn't have to be autobiographical, but that always seems to be the expectation. I don't know how to deal with that; I'm very interested in it as a problem.

SUSAN: I wonder if there isn't a further contradiction here between the expectations that surround women's writing and what women's writing often achieves? Masculine writing is traditionally equated with the desire for order and control, while feminine writing is perceived as being more fluid, more experimental, less structured. And yet this holding, nurturing function we have been associating with women's writing implies an order. I wonder if the difference is to do with the way this order is conceived of, with the way the housekeeping function is formalized or played out? The good mother, for example, offers learning opportunities to her children rather than simple admonishments of 'do' and 'do not'. It seems to me that the image of the red road in your piece, Nicole, provides this housekeeping role by offering a guiding path to the reader, an envelope, if you like, it is possible to explore *from* — rather than one that has been sealed down and delivered.

NICOLE: I think there is a contradiction here, a contradiction women have to face up to when they write. If they are aware of being *women* writers, if they are interested in that dimension I was evoking earlier, call it that dread word femininity or the female body or the maternal or housekeeping in the house of fiction, they also find themselves rebelling against the demand that notion makes, the exhaustion of self that somebody like Woolf went through when she was writing: Woolf spent herself, she was completely spent at the end of it. Colette did the reverse. Colette is somebody who manages it: she theatricalizes, she seems to be happily and endlessly writing about sex and pleasure and domesticity, giving you recipes to make chocolate and all the rest of it. So the one, Colette, plays the role and survives very nicely thank you, and the other one, Woolf, wears herself out. Of course, there are also women writers who would say I hate all this housekeeping, I hate all this domesticity, I want to be out, I want to be out into what is called the real world. I want to write about the stock exchange and war. What a lot of women writers in the past 20 years have done, in some form or other, has been to rewrite gender roles. I know that in my encounter between Rimbaud and Colette, I was very consciously turning the passive/active models around. In my story it is endlessly active and aggressive Arthur who, when found sleeping by the little girl, is deeply humiliated by this. He becomes sleeping beauty in a script that is none of his making and does what the little girl tells him to do. And yet strangely this does not demasculinize him. I find that terribly interesting — rewriting gender roles. How can what there is of a man in a man still be left standing if he ceases to be the active one out there doing big things? Also, how ruthless can you be? Carter in *Nights at the Circus* is very ruthless with Walser. She takes him through his paces, he is the clown, the Shaman, he is chicken, he is eaten. My Rimbaud also fears devoration. But neither his being passive nor his encounter with the female sex do him the damage he expects. The toothed vagina is *his* fantasy.

SUSAN: At the risk of being contrary I have to admit I find this argument over men writing women and women writing men hard to comprehend. It seems to me that everything hinges on context, on what and who it is you are writing about. I think it would be very interesting, for example, to explore the responses to a given situation across a range of different *people*. It seems to me that our gender identity is infinitely complicated, and much more complex than the simple division of the sexes would seem to suggest. A boy who has been over-protected, for instance, might react to the wolf in your piece, Nicole, in a very different way to a young girl who is used to dealing with animals. Of course, this is not to deny the reality of one's sex, or the way sexuality can motivate our responses.

One further point I would like to make concerning this aspect of writing the body has to do with its relationship to language and cultural training. A woman writer friend of mine has been trying to keep a diary of her pregnancy and the birth of her child, but has found it almost impossible to put her experience into words. There simply aren't the words to describe her experience. I think this lack in our linguistic capacities connects to another gap: the paucity of writing that evokes women's biological, sexual and erotic experience. Is it any wonder we are still operating under such taboos?

NICOLE: When I was writing my piece I had a lot of fun speculating about projecting myself into a male body, trying to imagine my character and how it would feel to walk around with a cock and balls. I wondered whether it would feel differently, whether you would feel braver or bolder or whether you would feel braver and bolder simply because that was what you were expected to be. Or did it feel like this because it was Rimbaud, who was so incredibly brave and bold and wild: was it this particular choice of character? When Rimbaud encounters the wolf at the beginning, it was delightful to me that he could calculate his chances of winning if he fought the wolf. In the event he knew he wouldn't win, and perhaps if I rewrote this now I could have a character who would know he was going to win.

I am beginning to think we are all in some part of ourselves androgynous, but that we can get so — for instance — feminized. I know this was my case, that I completely buried the masculine part of myself. I have become very interested in the idea that unless one has arrived at some kind of balance between one's feminine and masculine parts, one is never complete. As Jung came to see, if you're a woman you have to come to terms with your animus. Twice I have dreamt that I had balls. Once there was a wonderful shelf on which there were these beautiful balls in a pristine state, they were like white cheeses in cheesecloth lying side by side and really moist and totally fresh and I was terribly proud of them and delighted at their newness. Another time I dreamt that somebody was removing the obstacle or apparatus that kept my balls in place, like equipment you buy in its wrapping and when you remove the thing that keeps the parts from communicating suddenly they are free-flowing.

Again this was an absolutely delightful experience. When things begin to happen in your dreams it is very good. They're telling you something.

SUE: I love the idea, incidentally, that if writing can service our dreams then it is doing something beautiful.

I think it was Grace Paley, and before her somebody else, who said 'How do I know what I think until I see what I've said?' Maybe that's what I was doing in trying to write about the male muse — working with the unnameable object — not only in trying to address the male muse to get through to my subject matter, but also in attempting to write *about* the male muse, the unnameable; the two things happening side by side. It may also bear some relation to my determination and desire to get out of my own medium into another, and to find a model for the muse, which I could actually draw, draw from — and draw on. Perhaps I wanted to identify with him. Because what was very interesting to me in taking a male muse and drawing a male body was the extent to which the male model amusingly became not exactly directive, but determined to play his quite active part in the process of my drawing him.

One thing I liked about drawing a model as opposed to drawing on a muse in writing, is that the model doesn't talk, so that you do, when you are drawing, have this tremendous sense of authorship with all the terrible problems and pressures and anxieties and challenges of that, but you also have the sense that it is all down to you: that you are relating to the muse but you are totally responsible for the process. In writing, on the other hand, there's a sense in which your character comes to meet you and does a lot of the work for you once the process begins to run, and you get into dialogue with characters who actually begin to speak for themselves. When you start working in a new medium your responsibility as an artist faces you again. What was interesting was that it was a very awesome, overwhelming, exciting, frightening process, but it didn't take very long, once I had begun to work with the same

male model several times, before he began to interact and
to have strong views about what was happening between us
in terms of how I was relating to him as an artist and how
he was relating to me as a model, which didn't happen at all
when I drew female models. They would come meekly up
at the end of the session and ask if they could see the
drawing, whereas the male model got very interested in the
process as it was happening and had all sorts of things to
say about it. I tend to agree that it may be the case that try
as you might you cannot, even if you begin in artistic
terms, objectify the male because the male will not be
objectified.

NICOLE: You seem to be equating the male muse with a
male model. But traditionally for men, isn't the muse some
kind of winged creature appearing from nowhere, female
of course, who gives pleasure to the man and inspires him,
while the model is the silent woman usually from a lower
class who sits for him and lets herself be painted —
although sometimes as with Goya it is his aristocratic
mistress that you see.

SUE: I think that's right and I think that because I was so
determined to find a new way of, as it were, calling up the
muse, I went out in a very systematic way and found
myself actual models: if you like, containers for the muse,
suggestive forms. One of the disturbing and distressing
things that happened, as I have said in the piece, was that I
realized the models disturbed or excited me in relation to
how much they put me in touch with the muse. So that by
working with models what I was trying to do was both to
distance myself from the muse, and to bring the muse back
into play.

NICOLE: Do you think you are talking about excitement and
desire in relation to the model who is also the muse? I am
thinking of a poem by Du Bellay — which is about having
lost poetry — where he conjures a beautiful image of the
muses in the 'nuit brune' dancing for him under the rays of

the moon. It is the Renaissance. Obviously he wants to have it off with the muses, who become nymphs, the objects of desire. But if the muse-model in your case becomes the object of desire, does he then become active because if there is going to be love-making between a man and a woman there has to be activity in the man — there's less guarantee if it is the woman who chases after him. Do you think that has got something to do with it?

SUE: Yes, I think it probably has. Then I get anxious again about these confusions between the desire to write and erotic desire, and to what extent you need to remain in the house of fiction, and to what extent you are actually negotiating between your desire to make a work of art and other kinds of desire: at a very simple level, the confusion about whether what I am really experiencing is desire without an object, as opposed to the desire to make a work of art. And that's just terrifying and confusing and one is absolutely fired with creative capacity in that state and one writes a lot and feels terribly productive and creative. But then you're not really doing your best writing, making your best art, in that spirit. Or are you? Perhaps you are.

NICOLE: There is this ancient tradition of male writing whereby the male desires a female as a god desiring a nymph: Apollo and Daphne, or Pan and Syrinx. Pan doesn't get Syrinx, because she turns into a reed, so Pan picks up the reed and blows into it and makes music. Mallarmé writes 'L'Après-midi d'un faune' about this. Art comes out of absence; language out of negating the object. It is disappointed sexual desire that the male turns into music, into poetry. In the first draft of my story Verlaine did not get Rimbaud and began singing, he became the satyr, Hugo's *Satyre*, and his song liberated Rimbaud. You were talking about your desire and frustration, about your not getting sexual fulfilment when you write. You write when you find somebody unobtainable, out of that gap of desire. Again I wonder whether it makes any difference that one is female rather than male, since there would obviously be a lot of female activity in the love-making, but the male would not be in control. I am thinking of Jeanette Winterson's _Written on the Body_: it is interesting that it is called 'written' on the body rather than 'writing' on the body. She does begin by wanting to write on the beloved's body but ends up finding that love is written on her body, so she is really trying for a difference. The book is supposed to be ambiguous as to whether it is a he or a she, but that title in itself makes the narrator, the lover, very much a she for me, because I don't think a man writing about love would be writing about 'written' on the body, I don't think he would be trying to find the traces in his body of the loving. And again I am interested in that sexual difference.

SUE: I think that's right and I think that's where the anxiety and confusion occurs about whether — in this state of wanting to make the work of art the ultimate object of desire — this creates chaos and devastation not only in the work of art, but within the whole artistic process. Maybe a woman writer needs to be a very healthy, integrated person to tackle this actually very fragile, delicate process, and so the searing desire to make the work of art the object, because it's the only love object around, virtually demolishes the work. Whereas for a man in the same state it might be the making of the work. I do think that this is what I experienced and that it comes into the work itself. And yet there is also that warring desire to 'be a man', because the artistic responsibility is in some senses a very unfeminine responsibility: and one is always facing up to one's responsibilities and tapping this desire and using it with authority and staying in control, while at the same time being receptive, flexible, ready to explore.

NICOLE: Again I think of the Renaissance artists who _knew_ so much about desire and poetry and grief. I think of Du Bellay writing 'Je ne pleure, Magnan, je chante mes ennuis/Si bien qu'en les chantant parfois je les enchante. . .', about singing one's troubles, one's angst, and enchanting them in the process of singing. And that reminds me of

what Woolf says about the need to access the lyrical voice.
It is the lyric that saves you — but how in fiction do you
make it do that? There is very little contemporary fiction
that does that.

SUE: Well again, what happens is that you simplify; at least
I feel I've simplified, because in the novel I've been
drafting in the process of writing for this book there is a lot
of singing, there are songs all through it. But the problem
is that even if my character sings and there are songs
written into the text, is it *my* lyrical voice which I want to
release, or is it a substitute for it?

SUSAN: I was thinking of what we began with, this notion of
the (woman) writer's role as containing, holding, nurturing, and of how that might relate to the title we have
chosen. I was struck, while the two of you were talking, by
your insistence on the need to access an assertive, masculine part of the self in writing, and your equating this with
an active, masculine desire. It seemed to me that here were
two quite different shapes or energy sources: on the one
hand the passive container and on the other the driving
impetus of desire. It reminded me of traditional representa-
tions of the male and female sex and I wondered, in the
way Jung believed in the necessity of both masculine and
feminine, whether in fictional terms it might not also be the
conjunction of these elements that creates the work of art?
I can certainly see ways in which — if we interpret these
components in this way — I need both to be present in the
novels and stories I enjoy. When I read, I require some
form of envelope to give cohesion to the work, and yet
there also has to be a motivating energy that is of a
different nature to this holding function to propel you
through. I think this is equally true when I write.

SUE: And how would you translate that into the creation of
character? For example, in the male characters you have
created in your novel, what is the relationship for you
between those separate dimensions and what you do with
actual men in fiction?

SUSAN: First of all I am aware that I have to a large extent
skirted the problem in the work I discuss in my piece, since
all the male characters without exception are filtered through
the perceptions of my central protagonist. They have specific functions, and in this sense they are not characters so
much as products of the narrative. As far as writing male
characters in a more general sense is concerned — and at
the risk of adopting the role of devil's advocate! — I have
to say that I sometimes find it easier. I think this has to do
with what you were saying, Sue, about the complications
that can arise when the self is engaged in the fiction: if your
character is a man it can be easier to take him as an object.
I think I sometimes find it easier to work with a character
with whom I don't feel any immediate or absolute identification, since it becomes more possible to allow the processes that come into play when you write — the unexpected generation of new scenarios for example — to be
woven into the narrative, without feeling you have to
protect your character from any resultant humiliation or
hurt. It's a little like the feeling I sometimes have when I'm
watching a film. If I have identified too closely with a
specific character, I sometimes literally can't watch if that
character gets into difficulties. It is the same in writing. If
there is too much of myself in a character this over-
identification can operate as a brake, whereas, when the
character is more distant, I have a very different investment
in what happens to him or her. I feel much freer to experiment, and to allow the characters their own reactions
without automatically attributing mine.

Of course this distance does not have to come from
gender. In _The Aquarium_ for instance the protagonist's
exaggerated romanticism and lack of maturity often provided the same function. Nevertheless I do find sexual
difference can operate as a distancing device, and in this
respect I don't think I have gone as far as you, Nicole: I
haven't identified in the way you have with my male
characters, and I've unfortunately never dreamed about
balls.

One other point I would like to raise here is that it does seem to me there is a danger in the discussion we have had so far in our defining certain functions as male and female in ways that link so closely with sexual biology. Don't you worry that there is a danger of our broaching the problem of essentialism here? That this enveloping, womb-like space we have seen in women's fiction once again reduces women to a biological cliché, and that the active energy and desire we have equated with male sexuality confirms men in their usurped position of first sex? I think we have arrived at some important notions and yet I wonder if we might redefine these without recourse to a reductive biology?

NICOLE: I always get mad when one talks about biological essentialism, first because it seems to me a contradiction in terms and second because I see it as a permanent misunderstanding between two cultures, the French and the English. If you tell Luce Irigaray she is essentialist, for instance, she doesn't know what you mean because she is talking for ever about representation and culture and discourse — the discourse of psychoanalysis, the discourse of philosophy — and when she writes that our lips talk together, or whatever the phrase is, she is countering Lacan's 'woman cannot say'. The very pun about the labia 'talking' takes on ancient metaphors about female genitals as a 'mouth' — and a supposedly dumb one. The whole idea of *sex* talking is itself symbolic, is itself discourse; the phrase is a turning around and reclaiming of 'male' discourse. When people say if you insist on difference on account of the female body, female sexuality, then you are reducing females to their anatomy, this jolts me because anatomy is not destiny, though it does exist. It is part and parcel of culture, and cannot be envisaged outside it. *Ecriture féminine*, writing of the body and all the rest have been parodied out of all sense by people who are afraid of their bodies. It's not a matter of daubing your clitoris or labia in green, blue or red ink and then going over a huge piece of paper writing. That's what Yves Klein has done with his blue nudes, and that's a _man_ getting women painted blue to rub over a canvas. That's not writing of the body. That's a man using a female body for his brush.

Women's capacity for motherhood, the fact that women are or can become mothers, has throughout the centuries and possibly the millenia been used in all sorts of elaborate cultural ways we still only partially understand — despite masses and volumes written about it — to define women in a variety of ways and to relegate them, in the Victorian period for instance, to the life of the emotions. That is not biological, that is cultural, and it _includes_ anatomy. When one talks for instance of having 'balls' and of how this gives you an idea of courage, it is cultural as well as anatomical. When I was a child I was frightened of dogs and my little male cousins weren't. I imagine that had I been a little boy I wouldn't have been frightened. But one reason why I wouldn't have been frightened is because little boys were expected not to be frightened, while little girls were supposed to be self-effacing and not run and play games. That I was less strong is only part of it, part of a pattern. I don't think courage is a male or female attribute. I think it is constructs like these which are so deeply ingrained and go so far back into our psychic lives and the way we have been brought up that for a woman like myself to imagine having courage I have to imagine having a cock and balls. I have to imagine myself as a knight, then I put on my armour and access what has been a male image, although I believe there were female knights.

I think that talking in terms of biological essentialism is saying: stop writing about your bodies and start pretending you don't have a body or that you are somebody else. Writing about somebody else can be progressive though. I think that Angela Carter, for example, kept all those questions at a distance for a very long time, and then in her later work accessed more of herself through male and female characters, through carnivalizations, and so on, which to me _was_ progressive. That was getting beyond discourse and representation, beyond speech and images. I think that often when we want pure discourse it is for the sake of some impossible political correctness, and that in the process we sweep everything else under the carpet — and then we trip on the carpet. And don't we fall on our faces!

SUE: While you were talking I was thinking of Caryl Churchill's *Top Girls*, and of how she shows the pitfalls of trying to access the male part of ourselves if the male part of ourselves is conceived in terms of mythology. She's got females playing male roles in order to become strong women and they are very strong at playing these roles. There's the female Pope with the silly chair with the hole in it and the female business woman who is very good at being a female business woman. Then there is a terrible gradual collapse, and dreadful encounters at the end of the play between the 'successful' or well-paid female and the 'failed' responsible female who has taken on the problems of other 'failed' responsible — and 'successful' — females. It culminates in that absolutely mind-bending ending which shows the young woman of the next generation just standing in the doorway saying 'Frightening'.

SUSAN: I was interested in what you were saying, Nicole, about this whole essentialist debate being a cultural misunderstanding, how Anglo-American commentators have interpreted the writings of women like Luce Irigaray as literal description rather than literary metaphor. Something both our texts have in common is this interest in translation, the way meanings alter as they are set out in different languages. I have read your story in French as well as in English, and I am fascinated by how different the two stories are. I was wondering if you could say something about how you view these two texts, the one English and the other French? Could you say something about the processes involved in writing each, and the differences you perceive as you move between them?

NICOLE: I think this is a large and interesting question.

First of all there are the completely different connotations.
When you quote or half-quote Rimbaud in French everybody knows what's there. When you half-quote it or try to
re-write it in English nobody knows what is there. So you
have a world of connotations that play around every word
of the original that disappear when you translate. To take a
very simple example from the beginning of my text, my
character imagines his insides are like a map of the world.
His faeces, his intestines, are the black colonized parts and
he calls them his Antilles, his West Indies (there is an idea
of sugar crossing through his body which is itself his neo-
colonial fantasy: he's a white, French young man). The
names have different connotations: Antilles, which I liked
the sound of and which was very resonant for me, doesn't
mean anything in English, so you have to say West Indies.
But when you have said West you have said something
else, and when you have said Indies you have said something else again. So then do you name Jamaica? Well, why
Jamaica? It was never a French colony. You can't translate
it, so you have to rewrite it. But in doing so you lose a lot;
in translation I think you always do. So sometimes what
happens is that I simply start writing in the other language,
I write something else. It is the only way I can do it. But
that makes me very aware that there is one type of reality in
one language and another in another language. Especially
in literature where there is such a long history — a world
arises around the writing whether you are quoting or merely
revisioning. I can imagine that _Wide Sargasso Sea_ is not
popular in France because very few people have read _Jane
Eyre_ and the island race and class connotations don't easily
come across. The text changes from one language to the
other.

SUSAN: And what about the second part of my question?
How do you feel about the two texts once you have been
through the process? How do the two 'bodies' differ?

NICOLE: The French body is the more real, the more rhyth-
mical, the better anchored. But the English one so far has

gone inwards. I went to Plymouth to give a reading of the opening section and I got some very thought-provoking responses, in particular Peter Redgrove saying 'Has it ever occurred to you that the red road could have to do with female menstruation? Could it have to do with a different sort of blood from wound blood, from war blood?' Up to then for me the red road had been about the 1870 Franco-Prussian war, and the 1914 war that was to follow. What Peter Redgrove said hadn't occurred to me at all. (What a name in the context, incidentally! You'd have thought he'd been named on purpose.) What he said enabled me to rewrite the end of the tale. I read through *The Wise Wound* which is the book about menstruation by Peter Redgrove and Penelope Shuttle, and also Jung and Marie-Louise Von Frantz on the grail and female blood. So, in a way, all this went more easily into the English text, and now I have to translate it from English into French. The two texts have crossed. The first part is more French while the second part has integrated some Englishness, though they remain two different texts.

SUSAN: I was very interested in the image of the red road in your piece, and I think it would be fascinating to read it in terms of women's menstruation, women's blood. It seems to me that this demarcates a totally different journey to that conjured by the war-torn fields of Northern France and the blood of war. I was rereading Vera Brittain's *Testament of Youth* the other day, and I was again struck by the naivety of the young men determined to enlist and to measure themselves against the fear, violence, horror and death of trench warfare in the First World War. In Paris recently there has been what might be perceived as a worrying new twist to this male desire to confront death in a disturbing romanticization of the young man with AIDS: I am thinking of Hervé Guibert's book *A l'ami qui ne m'a pas sauvé la vie* — and particularly some of the reviews it gave rise to — and films such as *Les Nuits Fauves*. The trend can also be seen in plays like *Angels in America* which was at the National Theatre here, where the female characters are portrayed as either selfish or mad.

We have talked a lot about crossing genders and accessing different parts of the self, and yet one thing that strikes me is how little we have achieved as women in terms of instating an alternative red road. In a period of undeniable male self-doubt I worry that what we are experiencing is once again women's annihilation, and _not_ the possibility that there might be courage in production rather than destruction, that confrontation might be with life instead of death, that blood might be the blood of birth. I think it would be very interesting to discuss how we see women's position today in terms of the agendas of, say, 70's feminism, and what this in turn implies for women's writing. Can we as women writers counter these death metaphors and replace them with equally powerful images of life? Can the envelope be a womb in this preserving and generating sense? And is this what we as women writers would want to do?

NICOLE: It is terribly interesting that you should bring up men's fear of women in this context. As we get towards the end of this century, I can see signs of a revival of the decadent period of the end of the last century. There is Camille Paglia, of course — and don't the men who are bothered by feminism love her! She wants to revive as new the idea that Woman = Nature = Chthonian, sexual destructiveness. Old stuff in new drag, as over-simplifying as what she attacks as the supposed feminist equation: Woman = Good-Mother = Rousseauist Nature. There is an older book _Idols of Perversity_, full of images of women produced by men, in which women appear copulating with animals; as gulls, vampires, Salomes, threatening, castrating; there's a beheaded John the Baptist; and so on. The last _fin-de-siècle_ is full of such images, interpreted by Dijkstra or Gilbert and Gubar as acute male anxiety about their own identity, as fear of their weakness and therefore the projection of those fears onto their image of a _femme_ *fatale*, the destructive woman who takes you over. I don't know to what extent we are seeing a resurgence of the phenomena at present.

There is Robert Bly, who has such appeal in the US and now has some appeal in England, with his call to men to rally together in the search for good father figures and a reclaimed masculinity, and for escape from the choker mother. There is a drive towards male bonding and a revival of the Cleansed Frontier image, being men together in the face of the nature you conquer and bond with, as it were, away from the suffocating influence of women. It has an appeal to men who are undoubtedly having a very hard time in an age of recession, in an age of self-doubt, in an age of the collapse of ideologies, in an age in which people have forgotten the effects of two World Wars — the new generations have no memory of that. For these generations the second wave feminists are the mothers, who are seen, in books like Neil Lyndon's, as the villains of the piece, responsible for the evils that have befallen men.

SUSAN: It makes me very angry in this context when I hear young women proclaim that they are not feminists, as if feminism has become out-dated. As if feminism has somehow achieved its goals. And yet everyday I am reminded of the misogyny and crippling disabilities women face, even here, in the so-called First World. Even within feminism there is a sense that unless we can come up with a scintillating new angle or theory we are not making any real or valid contribution. Any attempt to return to the root questions that generated second-wave feminism is dismissed as old hat. And yet it seems to me that what we need now in the face of such hysteria is precisely a reintroduction and re-examination of some of the debates and agendas of the early 70's. But this need to be constantly original and modern prevents us from doing that — there is the feeling that because these ideas have already been formulated and argued over there is no further point in doing so: there is an assumption that the question is settled. And yet this could not be further from the truth. I wonder if this isn't where women's writing might again take up the challenge, using the resources of fiction to regenerate interest in these crucial debates?

NICOLE: I was thinking while you were talking earlier that we have gone back to what Simone de Beauvoir was looking at in _The Second Sex_ when she says men became the first sex because they learned transcendence, because they were forced to risk their lives defending their women folk and children, whereas women, because of their reproductive function, remained at home with the young. Women did not risk their lives for the sake of the group. And power has passed not to the sex that gives life but to the sex that kills. This is how she rationalizes the first and second sex. It seems to me that what we are seeing in films like _Les Nuits Fauves_ is a resurgence of this fascination with death. Despite a century of extraordinary violence, two World Wars, and all the attendant and monumental disasters of the Holocaust and Stalinist Russia, people's memory of what actual violence is like has faded, and violence has become what happens in Cambodia, or Somalia — somewhere else. People have become fascinated by it. And this desire by men to be tested in their courage and to be reassured in their virility through an encounter with death remains unappeased. I think this may be one reason why AIDS is being romanticized and even glorified when it is just appalling, just destruction, just terrible. And what I find worrying in feminist discourse is that its preoccupation with post-modernism in terms of destabilizing gender, destabilizing identity, destabilizing full stop, means it has little chance of opposing such a threat.

SUE: It does feel like a highly sophisticated form of skirting the issue, this construction of all sorts of variations on the destabilization model, with the idea that if you are able to produce a highly sophisticated, theoretical, water-tight argument then you have done the work. I worry about the kind of distancing effect this has, and about the notion that it is possible to be completely and totally theoretically reconstructed. There is a notion of performing a kind of theoretical acrobatics around very subtle, very potent, distinctions between subject and object, implying that there is a sophisticated resolution in bisexuality, when I don't think that position offers a resolution at all. The assumption seems to be that if you can produce the discourse then you have performed the political act. I just find that so deeply unsatisfactory. The notion that it is impossible to stabilize your identity sufficiently to destabilize it is something the theorists seem to have abandoned, because that is biological essentialism, that means going back to talking about menstruation and all the rest of it.

I think what has emerged for me in writing the piece — which, incidentally, has made me even more anxious about my relationship with my art than I was before — is the idea that it is possible to develop a discourse to explain your own position, vis-à-vis your own biology, your own art-making function, which seems to have solved the problem while in fact it has simply removed you from it. You have produced a discourse, but you can't touch the thing you actually need to touch. It reminds me of what Richard Ellmann says about Joyce's epiphany: it wouldn't necessarily have to be a moment of radiance, it could be a moment when language fails, a moment of darkness or breakdown of communication, which might perhaps end in laughter: that would be epiphanic. Just because we've found political explanations for some things, it doesn't necessarily mean we're getting any nearer to understanding what it means to be a female self. It's philosophy we're missing from, not political practice.

SUSAN: There does seem to be a consensus that for theory to fulfil its function it must not create but destroy.

SUE: Not necessarily destroy: avoid.

SUSAN: One of the questions we have raised in this discussion is why fiction might be important. It seems to me that there is an answer here. If the function of theory is to criticize, then generalize, it must always in some measure attack, destroy, avoid, if it is to attain its goal. This is the very antithesis of the way fiction works which, as it builds and peoples its worlds, envelops in another sense, and thus offers a different kind of learning, synthesis, knowledge.

SUE: But what you say astonishes me because the way you use theory in your piece seems very enabling and precise. It seems very enabling to you and very enabling to the reader as a way of understanding your work. You seem to have produced for yourself a particular kind of theoretical discourse that works very efficiently with your fictional discourse, so I am surprised to hear you say that.

SUSAN: And yet I don't feel I'm theorizing so much as attempting to see through the 'semi-transparent envelope' a little more clearly. I'm not trying to prove or disprove and I'm not concerned with generalizations, though I am interested in drawing out the connections. Is that the difference?

SUE: It's the 'semi-transparent envelope' that's the problem, I think, because why are we half stuck down? Why are we in this thing where we can lift up the flap and peep out?

NICOLE: I don't think we can peep out. I think as far as writing fiction is concerned it is the fact that it is semi-transparent that is important. For me one of the problems with theory is that it _pretends_ it is transparent or rather that transparency could exist; it acts, it speaks as if it did exist. I don't want to knock theory, because I think this is where feminism is most alive at the moment, and it is terribly important that it should be kept alive. The very dynamism of Feminist Theory proves that women have managed to establish the high ground, the high philosophical ground, and its discourses are certainly the most fruitful, the most interesting, the most self-generating at present. What I think is dangerous is that it becomes forgotten (because most of the women engaged in theory are women in an intellectual elite) that reality has not followed, that the fate of women throughout the world has changed very little and in some places it has become worse. In whole areas of the Third World for instance. What I find personally irritating about a lot of theory is that despite talk of diversity people write as if there were an unspecified common feminist agenda. Even the term 'woman' is discarded as heterosexist, and yet a consensus is sought in the march towards an ever receding horizon of greater and greater sophistication while the tone somehow assumes everybody else is following — or would follow if only they were wise enough to see how good this is. But at the same time what is being recommended is only for the head and leaves the rest of the body behind, and certainly the heart and sex, even though there is endless discourse about sexuality. Then you have the extraordinary turn around there is now in this drive to theorize the body and sexuality, as if in theorizing it you have somehow got it right, which seems to me an extraordinary piece of naivety. I think sex is messy, as human beings are, and no cops-and-robbers game is ever going to set it right. And that's where I think fiction, poetry, drama — all these other things women do and in particular feminist women — are so important, because in this type of writing there is body, there is materiality, and hence reality.

SUSAN: There is also the specific in fiction. It seems to me that the problem with theory is that in its search for generalizations it overlooks the specific. One of the difficulties I have with the current fashionable proliferation of theories of sexuality is that they fail to take into account the particular emotional journey that envelops the sexuality of each one of us. It seems to me that the advantage of fiction is that it begins with *this* envelope, and that, in the process of recreating its causes and effects for specific individuals, it arrives at potentially different conclusions — conclusions which may well have been left out of more generalized, theorized versions. Perhaps the difference is that theory offers the reader the pre-sealed envelope, whereas (most) fiction transfers the task of theorizing to the reader: it is up to the reader to discover the similarities and differences and to create from them, if they so desire, theory.

SUE: I got stuck at the point where Nicole was saying there is body, there is materiality, but it's not theorized. Then suddenly I got charged again with the idea of negotiating: actually in the act of writing, the process of writing. What do you do with the body: are you writing to create a position outside it or are you always necessarily writing through it? I'm struck by Nicole's image of the woman daubing herself with ink and wriggling around on a piece of paper. Is there a sense in which that is an analogy for what we must do, or is the fact that it is an analogy a way of saying we do something other than that? In that case, the other thing we do needs to negotiate with that analogous activity. But what is that other thing?

NICOLE: Well, perhaps I can give an example of how for me 'fictional' writing works differently from 'theoretical' writing. I am thinking of the first sentence of my story which, if I translate it into English, is 'I went under the sky, it was pale'. This came about because I had the idea of the red road and then a quotation came to me from 'Ma Bohême' by Rimbaud: 'J'allais sous le ciel, Muse et j'étais ton féal', 'I went under the sky, Muse and I was your vassal'. This got me started. I didn't want simply to quote Rimbaud and what came was 'J'allais sous le ciel' followed by 'il était *pâle*' because in my ears there was the echo of 'j'étais ton *féal*', there was an internal rhyme. But the internal rhyme crossed because 'pâle' has a mute 'e' (a French feminine ending) and 'féal' is a masculine rhyme. So I was already crossing genders. I only realized afterwards that what was also apparent was the notion that the road was made of blood. You might have thought this was obvious, but I had more the colour in view than the idea of blood. Yet already the road was beginning to drain the sky of blood. And the first line of 'Ma Bohême' is 'Je m'en allais, les poings dans mes poches crevées', 'I went, my fists in my burst pockets'. In French the pockets are feminine, a sort of feminine container, and he has burst them open; the liquid has drained out. For me the idea of vampirism is not only one of draining as so often presented in literature — the stories of vampires and pale people visited by Dracula — it is also the experience of periods and being pale and interesting and the strange cleansing pleasure and renewal when one has a period. The choice of 'pâle' introduced the idea of vampirism, which already contained this other potential I discovered only four years after the story was written when Peter Redgrove asked me, 'Have you thought about menstruation?'. I think this is what I mean when I say that when you write fiction all sorts of things go in, some of which are connected to knowledge you don't know you have. But you cannot theorize this.

I wanted to say something in relation to your piece, Susan, where you talk about happiness and the difficulty of writing happiness and how little there is in literature. It reminded me of the French phrases *les gens heureux n'ont pas d'histoire* and *on ne fait pas de la littérature avec des bons sentiments* — happy people don't have a history and you don't make literature with good feelings. I think there is a sense in which feminist fiction of the 70's and early 80's got caught on the horn of this dilemma: that feminist fiction would be about goodness or would be empowering to women or create a positive agenda or find a good new relationship to nature — as in Margaret Atwood's *Surfacing* — through accessing the deeper self. There were a number of sharp shooters in the midst of this. Angela Carter is very visible, also Fay Weldon, Kathy Acker and even Lisa Alther or Joyce Carol Oates. Come to think of it there were quite a few women writers who refused that goodness agenda. But I think it haunts theory — and the theory of fiction in particular — and it is still there in feminism: in facing up to issues like the cruelty of life and the fact that good writing doesn't come out of the search for goodness, it only comes out of an encounter with reality such as it is. And it strikes me that the dilemma is not just present in white women's writing. Alice Walker's work is positive and forward looking — not that there isn't value in that as there is in *Pilgrim's Progress*. But somebody like

Toni Morrison doesn't try to be positive in that way, she takes on board the actual encounter with viciousness, with child murder, with the goodies not being goodies but being both goodies and badies, even though they may also be the oppressed and the victims. She takes on board damage that is irretrievable. And that seems to me paradoxically more forward looking because anything truly positive comes out of an encounter with the fullness of life. If something positive comes out, this positiveness comes from truthfulness, not because it is empowering or good. I think theory must take this on, this idea of fullness. When one is told it is somehow good guerilla tactics to subvert everything one should ask 'what is one subverting _for_?' What world do we want to bring into existence, and what world is it _realistic_ to bring into existence?

SUE: Also I think the desire to destabilize is actually a desire to be all-encompassing or authoritative. It doesn't matter whether you are producing a theory about stabilizing everything or whether you are producing a theory about destabilizing everything, it is the implicit desire to be all encompassing that strikes me. I was thinking as you were talking of two novels, one is _Wide Sargasso Sea_ and the other is Joyce Carol Oates' _I Lock the Door Upon Myself_. I was thinking back to Luce Irigaray and the notion that when we are writing we are 'only' writing, and that there has to be a dynamic relationship between desire and the formation of the word. The word isn't flesh. So what you are doing is writing something into a position where you can touch it. I'm thinking of what Joyce Carol Oates' does in _I Lock the Door Upon Myself_ in describing a very passionate woman who just ditches everything to act out her desire, and as a result has a terribly tragic life. It's not until we turn over a blank page and see the figure '3' and read a new section that we realize that the narrator is talking about her grandmother and that written into this (but we, as readers, have to work to get it) is the notion of inheriting desire, inheriting behaviour, inheriting emotional psychic standards. Then the narrator begins to write about her own desire and her own destruction, and twice in the book she makes it clear that she is actually *re*telling a story: twice in the book she uses the phrase 'she locked the door upon herself' because, in the end, the grandmother locks herself away, like all the great heroines who are determined to live out their desire against the odds — Bertha Rochester, Miss Havisham; it doesn't work so they have to lock themselves away. There is a refusal to compromise, which is as much a refusal as Colette's — completely different — refusal to compromise. But what's so beautiful about *I Lock the Door Upon Myself* is that once this phrase — 'she locked the door upon herself' — has occurred twice, you begin to notice it and to think about its implications and about the relationship between the grandmother and the narrator. You then close the book and turn it over and there's your title: *I Lock the Door Upon Myself*. But the relationship between 'I' and 'she' has been played out rather than stated: it's very discreet.

I was thinking as well about Bertha, at the end of *Wide Sargasso Sea*, who literally stands in front of the gold framed mirror and lets the candles burn the face she sees in the glass, and the face is her own face; she is Le Revenant: the ghost of herself coming back into the present. In literal terms, or if this were realist writing, this wouldn't get us anywhere within feminism because she has to destroy herself to make her point. But this is fiction, so it's a glorious achievement, and it makes me think so much about the relationship between the word and the creative deed. The word is always in there, it has got to be, but what is its status within the equation?

NICOLE: Semi-transparent from beginning to end — like life — or like the ghost of life?

Sue Roe

Shelving the Self

Preamble

For a long time after I had written what I thought was the ending of my third novel, *Marianne's Monster*, I became incapable of writing anything that felt as if it had any 'take', any purchase, any singing tone, any note. Call it writer's block, if you will, but in the process of chipping away at my block, I discovered that the block was not only preventing my writing, it was preventing me.

I found ways of dealing with that block — melting it a little, chipping small slivers off it, moving it from place to place — but while I did so, my next project still felt very far off. In fact, the more I worked at the block, the farther off the next book seemed to become. I had a cast list, a few ideas, a couple of interesting minor characters — one in particular — but it all felt like a cardboard cut-out novel; the characters felt like ventriloquists' dummies. I discovered something: I could describe place, but not momentum. I could do landscape; occasionally I worried away at a bit of a portrait, but I had lost my dynamic.

It felt as if something was being stretched inside my head: a membrane being pulled across my brain. I now understand why people bang their heads against the wall: my skull had my novel wedged against it. I wanted to split it, to release whatever it was that had got jammed. I could imagine it: the remains of a plate of very old spaghetti, rammed up so hard against my brain that some of the strands were being squeezed through into other parts of my head. My brain extended from the surface of my eyes to the back of the cranium — that bit of bone that suddenly curves into the softness at the back of the head — and the entire structure had something cold and wet and rotting squeezed against it: my unfinished novel.

Paradoxically, I was becoming ghostly, haunted with this old, cold stuff. I stretched and stretched, until I felt as if I was made of something very fine, semi-transparent, like a moth's wing. I was grey and see-through and dried out. I walked around like a zombie, forgetting. I forgot everything. I forgot why I couldn't finish my novel. I forgot the time, I forgot to pay bills, keep appointments, I forgot what day it was. I had two thirds of a satisfactory book, and something else: the last section, which seemed obscene and offensive, revealing too much and concealing too little. Even my best friends didn't like it. Even my most cherished reader didn't like it. No one would say why. But the feeling I was getting was that I had gone too far: I had said too much.

My third section was about someone who had closed down, someone who wasn't really functioning anymore. It was the culmination of what I wanted to say about the effects of absence. I wanted to write about damage. Why not? What was I supposed to do, redeem my novel by cheering my heroine up? What would Shakespeare have done with Ophelia? Bought her a new dress? Got her to apply for a new job? Perhaps my heroine was a bit too much like me. Was that what was upsetting everyone? In that case, I had a problem: I wanted to write a novel, not a journal. Perhaps there is only so much the reader can tolerate, of exposure to the stripping process that takes place when you begin to peel a character's artifice away. Perhaps that stripping process really is offensive; maybe, having stripped my heroine of her disguises, I needed to find some way of building her up again: re-model her. I didn't mind, in principle, having another shot at section three. But what I hadn't bargained for was the extent to which my character had drawn on my resources and had exhausted me; left me vulnerable, frail.

It took ages for me to see, first that *Marianne's Monster* was not really finished; then to write a new ending; then to realize just how much and in what way *Marianne's Monster* had ended me. A part of me that is. It was written in white heat, quickly, revised efficiently. But then I went on. I wrote almost another entire manuscript, trying in vain to encompass more and more of what might have been Marianne's story in order to try to justify the ending I had written.

That novel had drawn on an aspect of me which I only

partially understood. It had taken what it needed of me, sealed itself up and left me shredded. Bleeding, almost. Red hot, turned inside out, without the remotest idea how to proceed. How to get out of what I had created, or how to get back into the house of fiction.

The house of fiction does not readily admit the self — at least, not with the immediacy of a painting or a poem. It is spacious, draughty, with a complicated geography. It displays, it conceals, and offers a kind of communication from room to room. It is peopled. It is no use thinking you can make a house of fiction out of the planes and lines of a single self. As the author, you have to reveal what you see, while effacing yourself: it is a difficult balance, precarious and fragile, a delicate tightrope to walk day after day, since the house of fiction requires constant, careful maintenance if it is to endure. The transpositions of feeling, insight and vision have to be sustained and connected. Kept warm, dusted, kept alive. Your relationship with it, as its creator, is tenuous, complex, subtle, utterly demanding. You are in it: you are absolutely stripped bare in front of it, exposed; yet somehow you are supposed to make sure that, at the end of the day when the lights are dimmed, the fire's blazing and everyone is sitting comfortably, it isn't *you* they see.

The house of fiction is not about selfhood, it is about the human condition, but not in the same way as a painting or a poem. It may be used to offer objective correlatives: George Eliot writes brilliantly about communication and separateness in *Daniel Deronda*: that is what *Daniel Deronda* is about, but it is also about Jewishness. George Eliot was not Jewish, and such aspects of her psyche as she needed to draw on for *Daniel Deronda*, to address the question of the relationship between communication and separateness, are not our concern. Why did Dickens make Estella so silent? What did he need to say about the relationship between displacement and coldness? We may speculate on this, but it is not our concern the way the state of Auden's heart is our concern when we read Auden's poetry. The model for Miss Jean Brodie, Muriel Spark tells us, bore in only some respects a resemblance to the original. But then she goes on to describe the model for Jean Brodie: they are barely distinguishable in all but a few minor, external particulars. In creating Miss Brodie, Muriel Spark has re-created her muse. This is what happens. But it is of only incidental concern to the reader.

The novelist's business is to hide the cracks. To make something architecturally convincing even if it is composed, over time, of a plethora of materials, a variety of styles. In the end, the thing must have a completeness, a wholeness and a unity which convinces, whatever we find when we strip bits of it away. Like St Paul's.

All this takes time, energy, hard work, the right tools. Sometimes we are not equipped, even for the attempt. Sometimes we are too exhausted even to try. Sometimes, try as we might, we lack the resources to make yet another edifice, yet another intricate, delicate, resounding structure. But if we care about our art we must do something. We must keep it alive.

While I was doing that — *just* managing to keep it alive — I wrote a piece of fictitious autobiography/confessional, whatever you will. I called it *The Dark Heart of the Rose*. It was the strongest thing I had written since I finished *Marianne's Monster* and I had planned to use it as the basis of what follows, but when I came to look at it closely, I realized it was very far from being anything remotely connected in style or shape or structure to a fictional narrative. I had written from the heart and it had *gravitas*, but it was not, would never be, a novel. After working in an improvised way for a day or two, I decided just to keep going and see what happened. What emerged was a flood of feeling about the character of Marianne I did not know I still had in me, and a frail glimmer of a new character; as well as the firm conviction that I had clearly needed to get out of the house of fiction during that time, to put my own house in order.

The purpose of this book is to offer some deep and sustained insights into what happens in the process of writing a novel. The *desertions* I will describe here — first, of my character, Marianne, from the novel to which she is integral;

then my own half-realized desertion from the medium of fiction — constitute one aspect of the mystery of that process. It seemed a rum kind of offering, but then I read the whole thing through again yesterday, prior to writing this brief introductory explanation, and last night had a powerful dream. I was playing the piano with tremendous verve and panache. There was music open in front of me, I think it was Tchaikovsky or Rachmaninov, perhaps both, but I wasn't playing what was written, I was interpreting. My own notes, however, were perfectly sound. My chords harmonized, my syncopation was ingenious, my performance was original, dazzling and — of the deepest importance to me in the dream — I was a technical virtuoso.

It is, then, at least sound, what I have to tell you. It is an accurate presentation of what happened to me after finishing _Marianne's Monster_: it's in key, it's on the note; it is as sound an analysis as I can offer of one aspect of the mysterious procedure which encompasses the novelist's encounter with her muse.

The Self

At first, you have to let the self through. The self begs to be let in and to be included. I want to rise up beyond myself, up to the place from which I can command this house of fiction, exert my mastery to put it in order and set it all in motion. But the self, sensing that I am about to be both drawn on and shelved, immediately becomes demanding. Attention seeking.

I have just sharpened a pencil, dusted a shelf and decided I was wrong to buy a bottle of Diorella: I should stick to Chanel No. 19; Roger & Gallet's Vetyver for the night and illness and hot mornings; Coco Chanel for a sudden, dramatic change, and Frangipani oil for the things I won't tell. I know what my shoes are: black suede Jackie Kennedy court shoes and black suede pumps. I have dusted a shelf, lifting and replacing my Greek statue and a friend's gift of a meditating figure. I am deciding what to wear this autumn: a thin wool jacket with glittery buttons and a new skirt I haven't found yet; it must be tight across the hips, then falling from the thighs in what look like pleats but are in fact slashes. I want to see myself: I am piecing myself together, a fragment at a time, starting with the outside. I am tuning up my instruments and sharpening my tools.

But I am not starting with the outside, not really. This attention to the outer layer has only begun after a long period of striving. My outer layer has been in chaos: like a suitcase full of clothes. A garment for every possible occasion, every eventuality, every conceivable event, as long as you are prepared to arrive dressed up as somebody else. Do you know the feeling? It is a feeling that can be splintered, fractured, by a small, physical act: standing beneath a foreign shower, feeling the water course across your own skin; passing the back of your hand across your eyelids and experiencing a small yielding in your eyes, a small relief. Sitting on the beach at sunset, thinking each and every one of these slung, untidy stones could be my bones. I am bleached, parched, emptied and undone; where shall I go from here?

This is tedious, wearisome, this relentless emphasis on self — but it has to be got through. It is like the pain barrier, or other barriers we can only imagine; the sound barrier, the speed of light. There has been a block: it descends on me the way people describe depression descending on them — like a black cloud (shroud, more like; a flopping, heavy, shapeless thing) — and I am trying to fight my way out of it. I have been trying for about a year. No image will rescue me, no metaphor will redeem me. I have images, I have metaphors, but they are static, jewels in a jewel box. Sometimes after many months of this stasis I become ill. I lie in bed and the mattress seems to undulate beneath me: I hear words, music on the radio which, if taken together, could add up to something. I don't know what. I am sick, I am empty, I taste the first cup of tea and I don't feel cleaned out or calmed, I just feel greedy. I want pot after pot of hot tea. I feel as if I have been starved because I have starved myself of my words, shape, line, tone: my design. But the paradox is dreadful — the more you starve yourself, the more blocked you become: you become stuffed with starvation, turgid with it. Swollen like a sausage full of paper, ink, characters, paragraphs, absolutely huge with it all. But nothing moves. There are no pains, no contractions, it has all stopped moving in you. It is terrible, and the only words to describe it are the commonplace ones. The phrases you attach to it are meaningless, in this context: 'The people who walked in darkness have seen a great light'. That kind of thing. You imagine yourself — literally, you actually imagine this, not as a metaphor, as an activity — pronouncing these words from a pulpit, listening for the sound of each consonant as it hits the far wall, bursts its small skin and makes way for the next: 'The people who walked in darkness have seen a great light'.

That great light would be my relief, that burst of light, that little burst of light. Where is it? I cry out in the night; I wake, breathless, from dreams of being suffocated in a passageway between two doors, both of them closed. I utter sentences in my sleep: 'I can't put A and B together'. It is all too literal. What have they done with my poetry, is what I am really asking. What have they done with my music, my vision, my sounds?

What have I done with my poetry, my music, my vision, my sounds?

When I speak about my poetry, I mean this: my dancing shoes, my light, my colour, my shapes. I mean the poetry of others: Diaghilev, Bonnard, Cézanne, Matisse, Rilke; the poetry that goes right out of me, that reaches right out of and beyond me in a great arc like a rainbow; the excitement I feel about making a new mark. Give me a piece of thick, rough, paper, quickly, and a stick of charcoal, I think if I touched that page now I could make a new mark. Up, across, down, down, with some sternness, some lightness and . . . so.

Nothing at all to do with my black suede court shoes, my Chanel No. 19, my desire to design myself. This is a by-product. The necessary waste product: important, in its own terms, all part of the organism.

But the novel I would write now if I could, if I could somehow inch all those conditions painstakingly into place, would be nothing to do with my appearance, taste, politics, aspirations, views. My *design* would be something other than that. A novel is an infinitely complex, empathetic organism. Unlike a poem. My poetry is its accompaniment, its backdrop and orchestration, its colour scheme and odour, its supporting aesthetics. So I cannot move into my new season's design without my poetry.

Can the Woman Writer have a Muse?

My poetry yearns for reciprocity: it heaves and howls for it. My poetry is as commonsensical as a novel, but it is flighty. It is as faithful as a novel, but promiscuous. It loves: loves like a madwoman or a madman. It shrieks when its love is refused, it has got to have it or die. It reads women's porn magazines and is addicted to Satie's music. Play it a snatch of Bartok in the morning and it will go stony-faced to hide its joy. It adores the French language and craves the warmth of a child. There are things it has seen — striped maternity dresses with great big bows over the bulge like American Christmas presents — which torture it. It wants to sing. It is utterly, utterly possessive: it will go to the end of sanity for its man.

Its man? Is my poetry a woman? 'Unless you speak my language I cannot love you,' it says.

'Take my anger, it is only a manifestation of my greater strengths and I want to give it to you, as a gift,' it says. Is it a woman then, this river, this electricity, fire, water, blood? This pen and ink, this sound I am making; is it female? More female than the body, more female than 'gender', more female than anything I can expose, except in words?

It refuses to accept — cannot live with — a muse who is not a lover, a model who is not sexually responsive. It seeks

muses, it is frantic for models. It is noisily incredulous when
other women utter statements such as 'but can a woman writer
have a muse?' Women on panels, with microphones, whose
work has been celebrated and misunderstood. There they sit,
benevolently enough, in their smart jackets, lined up on their
platforms, saying into microphones before audiences of hundreds, 'but can a woman writer have a muse?' My poetry goes
wild when it hears this. It smashes windows, hurls flints into
the sea, twists itself into agonized acrobatics. For God's sake,
it yells, have you never tried to draw the human form? I mean,
really draw it, I mean, draw it to you, your charcoal hot in
your hand, the paper like your worst phantom, staring you
out, have you never stood before flesh and blood and thought
about line and form?

What are you saying then, you women writers, what on
earth have you to tell? Will it outlast Matisse, Shakespeare, or
Cézanne? Has it ever occurred to you how sharp they will
need to be , your tools, your machinery? How _feeling_, the
bones and flesh of your own hands?

Oh, get down, I want to say to some of them. We have
heard you, you have been up there long enough. Now. Imagine a world where there is no light, no sound, no colour, no
line, no tone. Hush! I am talking about beginning at the
beginning. Why has the need to do so passed unnoticed?
What is it, Volumnia says to Coriolanus? 'Thou prat'sd and
prat'sd. . .' Do stop going on about it all, just for a moment.
You have forgotten how difficult it is. Some things have been
forgotten: the pain of love, for example. I am not talking
about irritation, frustration, the niggling difficulty of putting
your point. I mean the agony of ecstacy. After two hours of
drawing I say, 'I am tired now, I can't do any more'. That's
when I do my best drawing.

But I cannot do it if the model is motionless, I cannot do it
at all with a model who stands like a sack of cement, I need to
make my shapes by looking carefully at the lines he makes
when he moves. Then when I freeze him I remember them, I
can see those movements in his flanks, the curve of thigh and
shoulder: his form.

Sometimes my muse fails to enter my model: then I cannot draw. I rub away at my page and nothing is suggested, nothing emerges. My muse has deserted me again.

I speak to him. I call him, I stand there in my old cardigan, my feet on the ground, my charcoal in my pocket, gazing in despair at a bad drawing that will not live. I whisper to him, trying to re-invoke him.

When I am still, when he neglects me, when I do not hear his voice for many months and when I cannot feel him inside me anymore, then the black shroud falls around me like a sheath and I feel my bones harden and my fluids stop coursing and I stiffen. Last night I woke in the middle of the night and heard a story in my head — a narrative just uncoiling — it was a story I was telling him in my dream, so I knew I had to get it down.

I got up and wrote it, there and then.

Last night I wrote a story for the muse, today I dusted a shelf, sharpened a pencil and thought about shoes. I have bought a new pair — suede, with a little fold at the front — for drawing and writing.

'The people who walked in darkness have seen a great light.' Where does that come from?

Drawing

I continued. Sometimes with the muse, but mostly without. When he came back, he came back to haunt me. To remind me what I should really be doing; to show me that I was being evasive. I began to double-track. I began to dream up another project which would take me away from *Marianne's Monster*: perhaps I could make a new book, a light, amusing, vaudeville story, based on the idea I'd had earlier, that characters could be puppets, masquerades, ventriloquists' dummies: the work, not of a fully functioning artist, but of an *artiste*. Perhaps I could make a theatrical novel, a novel in repertory, with a barely-sketched, retiring little waif as its central character: Fragile.

I began making her up, and planning her awakening. At the same time I knew I had to learn to draw. Fragile, the ventriloquist's daughter who would take a whole novel to find her own voice, could emerge as I was drawing. My muse wandered in and out of _The Ventriloquist's Dummy_. He haunted that house, listening behind the walls, crouched at the wainscot, running his fingernails up and down the window panes to tease me when the rain beat a rhythm outside. I felt him brush against me, particularly when my characters sang. But he tricked me a little, whenever he touched me he made me sing in another's words: my characters sang Frank Sinatra, Françoise Hardy, Nina Simone. He waited at the piano while my character played and, when she got up to greet him, slid away. He was there, but he was peripatetic. Not stretched out against me, not asleep beside me, not grinning at me across the table, filling my glass, lighting my cigarette; always, always there, as he was while I wrote _Marianne's Monster_. Then he had hovered at my shoulder as I drew, he watched me make every mark, he studied every line. . . But I have got ahead of myself. Let me backtrack a little, and tell you some more about _Marianne's Monster_.

For a long time after finishing _Marianne's Monster_ I went on writing that novel. It's a novel I feel guilty about. It pulls its readers in close, then clobbers them. For a while I thought it was about incest, it was so painful. Only incest could offer this much proximity, innocence and guilt. It began to be a novel about guilt — I have only just realized — which is why I can see, now that I think about it in these terms that for a long time I thought it was about incest and Catholicism. It began as a book about missing persons, and perhaps suffered, or perhaps I suffered, from the fact that its theme presented itself too soon. It was also, in a small way, a novel _in memoriam_, and that is as difficult to work with as writing to celebrate someone alive. The objects that throw themselves into relief, that present themselves as images, accessories, become too fixed when you are mourning someone real. They resist translation, and you need to translate all the time in fiction, in a way you don't in poetry. To turn Margate into Cleethorpes would make nonsense in a poem; to translate a journey with one's uncle into a journey with one's character's father would be a dubious kind of move for a poet; novelists make that kind of move all the time, it is the stuff the art of fiction is made of.

The dynamic of that novel led me towards grief and that, of course, is one of those blank and spacious human experiences which gets in all over the place. My heroine buckled under it. She crumpled and gasped for breath, but the trouble was that after I had finished I kept thinking, surely mere grief would not have flattened her like that. So I went on inventing crushing scenarios for her. I raped her, I put her in an incestuous relationship, and then I incarcerated her. All this time, the novel was nearly finished but I was burying it under these post-scriptum monsters. The typescript grew and grew, and I felt worse and worse. I couldn't get a sense of my structure, I had jeopardized my pattern but I still felt that there was further to go, there was still something else to be divined, deep, deep down in the soil of my book, deep, deep down in its dark heart.

I think it is possible to be driven mad by your creation: certainly *Marianne's Monster* and now the two new possible variations were driving me to distraction. Oh, outwardly I could pass myself off as relatively normal, though everyone told me I was drinking too much. Come to think of it, people did start asking me if I was under a lot of pressure during that time. 'No?' I said. I got into the habit of putting away a bottle or two of red wine on a Sunday afternoon and ringing up the sorts of people who can usually take it. 'It's Marianne,' I'd say. 'I think she's got to be mentally disturbed. I have just written her into the bin. Oh God, I think this is a novel about mental illness.' I got quite a stern response to this on one of my Sundays. 'Be careful. That's dangerous stuff. I'd put it away for a bit if I were you.' Oh, you mean it's *it* that ought to be put away. . .

The fact was, the material I needed wasn't in me yet, so I

couldn't get it on to the page. There had to be a solution for Marianne, but it simply didn't exist among the flotsam and jetsam I had been shoring up for her. I was trying too hard, with too few resources, it was like trying to climb a mountain wearing the wrong boots. I did what I always do when this happens — though I resisted it for as long as I possibly could, because I knew damned well how strenuous, how demanding this move would turn out to be — I changed medium.

Looking

I knew what to do one November afternoon in the Royal Academy. I had to paint and I had to draw, to somehow get my head — and my arms, voice and fingertips, everything you need to write a novel — round the human form. That afternoon I had gone to see an exhibition of Egon Schiele's work. A colleague of mine had a postcard of one of his paintings on her wall, and it spoke to me: the model on her back, knees drawn up, face turned towards the spectator. Now I can see that this is where Marianne needed to be; where she thought she was. My characters always long to model, it is just something that's always there, though it may not be stated. Or perhaps Marianne just needed to expose herself. Properly. Completely. I went along to see what I could find out about Egon Schiele, and when I got there I roamed around and got myself from a small purple and gold flower, Klimt-style, through all the Wally Neuzil studies and thence to gloriously copulating couples, and I stood in the middle of the Royal Academy and laughed out loud. I thought, here's my direction: this struggle. Woman as object to woman as subject: his life's work, though not necessarily conceived by him in those terms.

He used glue, I learned, to give the paint body; he applied lipstick directly to the canvas. I became fascinated by his materials: what was it he used, to translate, to transform? Lipstick. Glue.

I bought canvas, I bought paints, I bought lipstick, I bought glue. I bought every book about Egon Schiele I could lay my hands on. I went to art shops and talked to people about Egon Schiele. One man in a shop in the Charing Cross Road kindly spent the afternoon explaining about his use of green. I took myself off to the local park on Saturday afternoons and read my books about Schiele, varying them with a little Iris Murdoch, for light relief, and a lot of Rimbaud, whom Schiele had tried to emulate by writing poetry.

Schiele fascinated me and, for a time, obsessed me. Why? Because his draughtsmanship — the skilled use of line, the ruthless regard for accuracy, the spare, austere workmanship — touches the raw nerve of the sitter. At first glance we see the model *in extremis*: acutely desirous, lustful, suffering, totally exposed. And then, when we follow the line, pay attention to the proportions, it becomes clear that he has achieved this not through exaggeration but through *economy*. Schiele draws the sexualized self, from head to toe. His sitters are stretched to the limit, sometimes by leaning, leering, parting their legs, baring their asses; sometimes simply by sitting still with their hands in their laps. His portrait of Arthur Roessler is almost electric with barely contained lust, for money perhaps, or possession, ownership or social elevation; the desire to *hide* himself. No matter what — that portrait surely gives us more of Roessler than Roessler was ever aware of expressing. Schiele's portraits of babies are of creatures newly spun, alarmed, disorientated, beating the air like moths with battered wings, wide-eyed at the bewilderment of being out of water. His portraits of Gerti show the innocence of a little sister, a sexed creature, tantalizingly warm and close but other: of a different, powerful, taunting gender. His portraits of women are red hot, livid with life.

I tracked it all through, by reading all the analyses of his works, all the biographies; studying all the sketch books: the loss of the father, anger at the mother, desire for the little sister. I marvelled at the child's drawings of trains in the station at his native Tulln, where his father was station master; he would sit for hours with his sketch book, drawing the trains through the window. I watched Gerti take shape, as the early drawings of her become more sophisticated, with the emphasis always on line: as the art develops, the lines appear to be simpler, to carry more, with the toning always in blood reds, gangrenous greens, the use of yellow and blue that reminds us that flesh is always moving from life to death, that the life-line is tenuous, that skin, at the hands of a great master, becomes almost transparent: his figures are fighting with their bodies, howling to get out; screaming to find a way in.

He drew himself in mimed poses, twisting the body, stretching himself; taking to extremes — and taking seriously — the dilemma not only of selfhood, but of the responsibility of the sitter. Hold a pose for five minutes and you will see what I mean. The muscles ache, the skin pulls, you are all body, all flesh and blood and pose. A shape in the air, you are stripped of all the usual ways in which you present to the world your story of who you are. Display your hands, for five minutes, one resting on the other perhaps, and you will discover you have _hands_. They have bones, they go from cool to warm; in your right hand you are caressing five knuckles and a weight of bone, and your left hand is heavier than anything else in your body. Modelling or drawing any part of the body is like repeating one word over and over until it begins to sound malformed: it detaches itself from ordinary language and has a sound, a weight, a texture, a _lack_ of ordinary significance. A new weight; a weightlessness.

He painted white light around many of the heads, including his own; it has the effect of raising his figures up, making them luminous. When he retreated to Bohemia, in 1912, and sketched the local urchins, he was imprisoned for obscenity and his sketches of himself in sackcloth and ashes are of winged creatures, tangled up in their own membranes, fighting to beat their way out of their just-visible webs: the pencil and watercolour sketch entitled 'Hindering the Artist is a Crime, It is Murdering Life in the Bud!' is the sketch of an angel: poignant because it is _clothed_. The face of the hounded, haunted artist is contrite, bewildered; out of his element above the voluminous drapes and folds of his covering. He is almost a winged creature. By imprisoning the artist, by burning his sketches, society is disguising his humanity: that which he strove to expose by ceaseless hard work, the struggle with seeing; the refusal ever to let himself become invisible. In 'For My Art and for my Loved Ones I will Gladly Endure to the End' he is tangled up in pencil and paint; his hands, clawing at a semi-transparent film between the drapery and us, are almost deformed with the effort of trying to peel himself free. Here, as in the drawings in which the figure performs fellatio on himself — in which Schiele becomes the object of his own desire — he yearns for himself; the authorities have shut him away from himself and he fights like a moth beating against a flame. His crime was to have searched, *in extremis*, for himself. 'Certainly,' he wrote at this time, 'I have made pictures which are "horrible"; I do not deny that. But do they believe that I like to do it or did it in order to act like a "horror of the bourgeois"? No! This was never the case. But yearning too has its ghosts. I painted such ghosts. By no means for my pleasure. It was an obligation.'

This is succinct, clear, beautiful. But usually when he wrote, he said too much. In words he exaggerated, and knew nothing of economy. He fought to get out of prison, he got out; he went on drawing. There was a change: liberated from prison, the membrane of censorship *almost* visible in the prison drawings now punctured, he emerges with a different vision: now he wants union. He dismisses his faithful model of years' standing, Wally Neuzil, and takes a wife, whom he transforms in paint from a doll-child to an orgasmic woman. In his paintings, he is entwined with her: one flesh. He paints more children; Edith becomes pregnant.

As Edith lay pregnant and dying of influenza, he sketched her: one last, desperate attempt to catch her life, and make it go on beating. Soon afterwards, he caught influenza too, and it killed him. Up until then, he has caught and transcribed and displayed it all: the struggle, the stretching of life to fit him; the refusal to be covered up, hidden or disguised; the determination always to come out with it. It can all be read in the work. In line, light, colour, tone.

I identified with him. Not with the models, with him: with the career of that struggle. The desire not just to make life, but to *show* it.

I hit on my mission in life, in the Rotunda café, in Brighton, over a tomato sandwich and somewhat grey-looking capuccino: I would do out his life in verse, the way spinster ladies did out clergymen's in Victorian times. I would do out his life in verse and I would learn to draw.

Poring over a picture of a masturbating model, I looked up and recognized my friend Molly passing with her baby. She sat down, tucked the baby under her jumper and we fell to discussing my problems with Marianne and Egon Schiele. 'I'd love to do some more teaching,' said Molly, a fine artist. 'I'll teach you to draw. What do you want to draw?'

'Flowers,' I said. 'And the human form. The thing is, I've done flowers before, but I'm not so hot on life.'

'I'd jump in at the deep end if I were you,' said Molly. 'I'll get you a model, shall I?'

Here was the problem: Marianne was blocked. I was blocked. My relationship with my character was like the papery bit of a concertina; it could make notes, but there was something trapped somewhere in the breathing. 'We'll start by sharpening up your observation,' said Molly. Beginning the following Thursday, with a box of charcoal, a wobbly easel, a bottle of wine and — just to begin with, by way of a rehearsal — an almost-blown rose, I embarked on the painful, frustrating, sometimes excrutiating business of discovering the difference between looking and really paying attention — *really* looking. Marianne crept soundlessly into the shade somewhere and closed her eyes, relaxed her exhausted limbs, and slumbered, biding her time.

Fragile appears to have fallen by the wayside. I am backtracking a little, now, in an effort to make things clearer, though there will always be some things which will recur unresolved. I am coming to Fragile.

In and Out of the Inferno

Molly and I alternated work with recreation. We went to the park with the baby and played hide and seek; he emptied my purse for me, and played with my change. Then we redistributed all the coins into different coloured plastic pots. We had a good laugh about this, especially the bit about tipping them all upside down and losing coins in the grass. After a while, the baby stood up, bent down and grinned at me, posterior skywards, the little round face beaming between his legs. I said, 'Passion is wisdom, Molly,' apropos of a story she had been telling.

A large woman in a green striped dress and pink glasses materialized at that moment, at alarmingly close quarters, and handed us a plastic frog in a plastic car. 'Oh, thank you! Thank you!' exclaimed Molly. 'I'd forgotten all about Frog. Just think! We could have left Frog behind!'

'He was over there,' pointed the lady in green, thoughtfully identifying the exact spot.

We pocketed Frog, we stacked up coloured beakers, and I assembled what remained of my change. The baby took charge of the buggy, and Molly carried the plastic pots. All the time this was going on I was thinking about making a new novel: a novel about Fragile, the frail adolescent; daughter of the female artiste, the ventriloquist. All this time, I was trying to make a new book, an engaging one; a distracting little story, which would peep upside down between its legs at me, a story that would play. *The Dark Heart of the Rose* (my sketch book, which I later discarded) with its desire for new, pure, uncomplicated birth, had bred Fragile. Meanwhile, Marianne lay face to the wall. Slumped. Drunk. Drugged even. Ugly. Debauched. Very, very powerful. Studiously ignored.

I wrote an entire novel — *The Ventriloquist's Dummy*, Fragile's book — to avoid having to think about her.

I knew Marianne wasn't finished, but everything I was writing about her seemed to make her *less* finished. I wanted to write a novel about a painter, but what do you say? To write such a novel you would need to write about the work. I didn't know enough. To write a novel about a painter I would need to learn to paint. I did want to learn. But there was something nagging at me. I was making all sorts of neat-sounding equations, but there was something here that didn't add up.

And there is something else for me to contend with, now, in writing *this* narrative — the one you are reading. I have begun to introduce something else: another whole, new temporal dimension. When I peer backwards at my troubled novel, not the one that belongs with Satie or Debussy (*The Ventrilo-quist's Dummy*), but the one that needs Holst, Verdi's Cho-ruses, Bach's organ music, Franck, when I peer backwards at my monstrous book, I'm like the baby peering playfully upside down between his legs. I worry that I could never quite get back into its mood, its atmosphere, its voice, its song. I have lost the look of it, the sound of it. I need to read it again to get that back. Writing about how it came about, I can never quite give you the atmosphere of that coming, I can only look back and say, there, that's where I was then. Perhaps it's this that doesn't add up.

The baby peering backwards at me, upside down between his legs. What is it that children are doing, here, with this familiar contortion, this happy sense of flip-side up that they practise so soon after learning to walk? What is this, then: practice for sex? Or is it some deep emotion recollected in tranquillity? Or some deep recollection, in this instance, of life in the womb? Look: I can pretend to be a foetus again. But this time I have my feet on the ground, I can play it through like a game with you as a participant; this time it is amusing; this time I am in control.

If I look backwards at Marianne in that way, which may be the only way I can, now, look backwards and upside down at my invention, will you play?

I will have to do something about this breathlessness, this rushed feeling, always feeling that I must whip from one point to the next, that I can't *get down*. Is there a flurry of panic just for one moment, as they forget how to get up again? I can't get my feet quite on the ground. I can't quite stabilize this.

I was curled up, with Marianne. Curled up, waiting. Moving gradually forward, one step at a time, into something else: a new technique, a new mood; learning to cut deeper. But one is in the dark with that. It is all black as carbon. Your vision is impeded, you are floating around in fluid, you have grown into something with planes and masses; you are no longer, as you were writing your first novel, a speck; no longer, as you were with the second, an egg, bouncing from cell to cell, feeling things 'take'; multiplying, multiplying. With the third, it all begins to feel very different; it is all grown-up stuff. There are fingers and toes to think about; fingernails and toenails. New shapes are emerging and developing at different rates, sometimes alarmingly. With Marianne I felt a different kind of eroticism: blackly rooted. Deep red and uncontrollable. Writing my previous novel, *Masquerade*, I drank a lot of white wine. Writing *Marianne's Monster* I drank whiskey. Something happened to my imagination. It reared up in the night and touched me. I could feel its chilly fingers against my skin. It shrieked. It howled. *Masquerade* had sung its own music; Marianne screamed.

And was it *my* eroticism, then, my screams, my own monster? I wonder. I wonder if I touched myself too closely in that book; I wonder if I got too near myself. I abandoned myself to it and lay there, curled around the blood and guts of this thing, this vision, this invention, this art, and felt as if it was all very dark in there, mysterious: hot. I think that is the farthest into the fire I want to reach, but when you have reached that far into your furnace, pulling out is difficult. Pulling out is excruciating: you have been burned.

You are completely alone with it. No one sees that you have burned yourself badly on your own invention, no one sees quite how, or why, you are in pain. While you are burning up, it simply looks most of the time and to most people as if you have simply gone off on the wrong track. What were you doing in the furnace anyway? If you can't stand the heat. . . There are easier ways to write a novel. One of your friends is on page eighty-eight whereas the week before last he was on page seventy. In between he has gone

back and forth, writing and discarding, writing and discarding. . . Oh, it is all very irritating. But it is not consuming
him, he is not lying on the floor rolling around in a rug with
the flames licking. . .

It occurred to me (and to others) that perhaps I was depressed. Was I actually in the creative inferno, or 'just'
depressed, for heaven's sake?

I was in the creative inferno. If I stopped believing this I
would have to stop letting this thing flare up, and then it
would fizzle out like a damp squib and all the pain would
have been for nothing. Let me tell you: when it's like this, the
one thing you cannot do is 'put it away for a while'. No way.
It is a mistake to try. You can only stay in it or around it.
Right bang in the centre, or teasing away somewhere in the
vicinity. Onstage, or hovering at the stage door. You can
perform it or you can watch it. The one thing you cannot do is
put it to one side and go off and read some other lines in some
other play somewhere else. It's no good slouching away with
your head down, or flouncing off with your nose in the air.
You have got Marianne onto the couch and she is now your
responsibility. Somehow you have got to get her out of here
alive.

Let me give you one tip, in passing: don't let anyone tell
you your novel is finished when you know it isn't. Something
more complicated than the process of finishing may be happening. Perhaps your book is finished, but you aren't. Aren't
finished, that is, with the inferno. There is purgatory to come,
before paradise.

Purgatory

I stayed in that most excrutiating of places: half in, half out.
Not knowing whether I was coming or going. I am not there
any more (I said to myself) you must understand this. I am
making something new. There is Fragile to attend to: there is

a new character to be invented, a new book to be made, a new house to be put in order.

Thanks to Marianne I am out of it (I kept telling myself). I am elsewhere. I am in the throes of deciding whether the new thing I have been trying to make is over-ambitious or not demanding enough. I keep seeing glimpses of some essence I want for it; occasionally getting a strong sense about the *stuffs* I want in it — the objects, the material — but something at the centre, the vein running straight down the middle of it, is wrong. It is out of true and out of time, yesterday's papers. I have half a new thing and half an old thing on the stocks. It all needs weeding. They say weeds are flowers in the wrong place: well, some of my material doesn't belong here. Is that why Fragile feels *so* fragile? She is a reed in the wind, she is all blown and lit and electric, and I cannot have her lose that quality. In the novel as I have conceived it so far (I am talking about the new one, you understand: *The Ventriloquist's Dummy*), Fragile will toughen. I cannot have this, I must not sacrifice her delicacy, her cut glass quality. I know you want me to finish telling you about Marianne so that I can get onto the business in hand: that of explaining how I got as far as Fragile. I am coming to that. I am coming to Fragile. But look — something has happened, which is useful, to say the least. In writing about Marianne, I have seen something about Fragile, something very important about her world and about the world I am making for her. *Reculer pour mieux sauter*, they say. I am afraid none of this is very tidy, for the time being, I'm afraid I shall have to ask you to live with this stop-start, replay-fast-forward stuff, for a while. I hope you can forgive me. We will make a shape, in the end, we will make a shape.

I had to separate Marianne from myself. This was the difficult bit that felt like putting my hand in the flame — my body in the flame — then taking it out again. What was it Julia Stephen is reputed to have said of Stella? 'She is the other part of my soul'? That's what happened to Marianne and me. I over-identified, perhaps. I wasn't very strong at the time, what with one thing and another; I just wasn't entirely strong enough to let her have an identity of her own. No wonder she kept on giving up the ghost. No wonder, moreover, she got so angry. My character hated me, in the end she began to despise me, she railed and stormed against me until she had me, one Sunday afternoon, wimpering on the floor demanding to know what on earth I had done to deserve this. Well it was, after all, a fairly heinous crime: I had neglected her. She suffered, I suffered, we both suffered. It was a fairly typical difficult mother/daughter relationship. I suppose a bit of me just could not let her go.

Looking back on it now, it seems to me that I just wasn't ready to lose her. Something had to happen from outside; it couldn't happen between Marianne and me, we had absolutely drained each other dry.

I had to get out of the house more. I had to get out and *do* something. I don't mean earn a living. I don't mean concentrate on my job, get divorced, have a baby, throw a party. I don't mean anything like that. I mean I had to get another angle on Marianne. This I knew. This I could see clearly. What was difficult to decide was: by getting a new kind of purchase on Marianne, or by getting a new kind of purchase on me. I use this word flippantly, without much thought, but it's not a bad one. Getting a new angle on your novel can come expensive. For me it involved: art materials, an easel, paying a teacher, paying a model. Drawing books, paints. Clothes, make-up — and several abortive attempts to change my perfume. To name but a few items of expenditure. I wasn't *equipped* for Marianne, I wasn't up to her. I had to somehow reconstitute myself to launch this heroine, this new model and new character, this creature of fire and earth and salt and blood, this highly erotic creation I had turned up from somewhere out of the depths of myself. She lay quietly on the couch and slumbered, while I reconstructed myself. It was only one possible solution, but I had got to the point where I would try anything. I couldn't keep Fragile dancing while Marianne still lay comatose across the dance floor, one red shoe upturned against the wall. It was after hours, everyone had gone home, even the band, but Marianne was still slumped across the floorboards. I had to do something about getting her out of the picture, otherwise Fragile wasn't even in the running. Fragile wasn't even in with a fighting chance.

I have, now, got very near the point at which I ought to be able to tell you a story. It strikes me that by now I should more or less have prepared you for the lightning tour from Egon Schiele, retrospectively back through Marianne and on, through the life-drawing to Fragile. It is the life-drawing, I realize, that is bringing me up short. It is huge, life-drawing. It is an enormous, complex thing. I am not quite ready to embark on it and at the same time, I have just begun to realize, I am itching to do it. I have got to get before an easel again in order to get you from Marianne to Fragile. This is where Molly comes in. We were sitting in the park discussing models: which one to book. That's when the baby did his peering-backwards-between-his-legs act; the difference between that baby and a life-model: the baby's *glee*.

I will get back to the beginning as soon as I can. It shouldn't be too long now. Sooner or later there will be a story moving forward at a manageable pace, with a consistent thrust and a coherent design, which you will be able to get your bearings in. With luck.

I keep digressing. But this is in the nature of the material. There will come a point at which I'll be able to move forward.

Normality has resumed. I have to keep reminding myself of that. I am changing my life. It is not like it was with Marianne anymore. I am moving on. I am organizing my life to reflect this. I have put my flat on the market. It sounds such a bodily act, that: I can imagine edging it out of the back of a Volvo Estate, draped untidily in a blanket — right a bit, left a bit, steady does it — and then heaving it onto a stall already littered with old gate-legged tables, umbrella stands and broken chairs. Not a bit of it. A man called Derek comes round with a small machine which he points at the walls. It lights up. What does that do? 'Measures', he replies. What, without actually touching anything? 'Remote control', mutters Derek.

He steps over your piles of books, your fold-away spare

bed that you have never been able to work out how to fold away, your art case, your brief case, the letters piled up against the door for you to remember to post them; he trips over your phone lead; he snaps his machine shut. 'Right-oh', says Derek. That's it: your flat, once Derek gets back to his office, will be 'on the market'. 'Will you be in later?' he asks. What, in case lots of people want to come round and view it today? 'Well, I might have one or *two*. . .' suggests Derek, a shade non-committal. Anyway, the great advantages of all this are two-fold: firstly, it means you really are moving on. Secondly, it means you will have to be in a lot, at least for a while.

I nipped round to the hardware shop and got a spare set of keys cut for Derek, and a new 60 watt bulb for my desk lamp, just in case. Standing there with all those men in frayed T-shirts queueing up for screws, I can tell you I got a real sense of control over my life. On my way back I waded through Waterstone's to have another go at solving the mystery of Muriel Spark's autobiography. It has been reviewed every-where, extracted in the Sundays, advertised here, there and everywhere and yet not a copy is to be found in the shops. I've been attempting to get to the bottom of this for a while. I began in Dillon's Piccadilly. 'Who?' they said. 'It should be under S.' It was not under S, it was not in the pile of 'new titles', it was not in biography, but it was on the computer. 'Oh', said the assistant. 'That means it hasn't come in yet.' I passed swiftly along to Hatchards. They had it advertised in the window but had never heard of it. I could order it if I wanted to. I got a tube and tried Dillon's in St Martin's Lane. There they were most efficient. 'It's called *Curriculum Vitae*', said the assistant, actually talking as she walked about the shop, . . . 'and it'll be just. . .' — she stretched out a practised hand — '. . . Oh. We must have sold out.'

Waterstone's hadn't got it either. They did, however, have Laforgue's poems, a near-miss until I found that the transla-tion of *En Bateau* was entitled *Boating*; and Stephen Spend-er's *Journals*. 'I am going to keep a journal because I cannot accept the fact that I feel so shattered that I cannot write at all,' I read. I devoured a bit more on the way to the cash desk: 'Today I read in the papers a story by Seymour Hicks of a request he gave to Wilde after his imprisonment, to write a play. Wilde said, "I *will* write a wonderful play with a wonderful dialogue." As he said this, Hicks realized that Wilde would never write again.'

The car had ten more minutes to go on its voucher, so I used the time profitably in Ryman's. I bought a telephone message book and hovered about among the notebooks. It was the word notebook that bothered me: either that, or they had lines, which I can't abide. 'Notebook' would be too promising; so, moreover, would 'journal'. My new blank book is black with a red binding, on its cover the word 'Drawing'. I definitely need to start again with Fragile and I had to have somewhere I could record that note I suddenly made to myself a few days ago, while I was in the middle of writing this: 'She, Fragile, is absolutely the main, the key character.'

Digression. More digression. Anything to avoid going back into the inferno. Anything to avoid Marianne.

On the Rocks

Fragile is gaining clarity, becoming more distinct. So, too, is Marianne: what is becoming hazier is the area of dense undergrowth which exists between them, the area I think of as 'the drawing'. Creating order out of chaos does not involve putting chaos in order. Each of their respective stories must have a clear, central idea. I used to think the central idea in *Marianne's Monster* was incest or perhaps the impact of absence. Now I am beginning to wonder whether it might not be lust. Fragile's is altogether different. What is the central motif, the figure in the carpet, in the novel I am working towards? Do you know, something is beginning to occur to me. I am beginning to wonder whether the central idea for Fragile may not be that of *clarity*. Or claritas, perhaps.

Claritas. Now that is complex stuff. There may be a lot of undergrowth, a great deal of connective tissue to cut through if I am to disembarrass Fragile of all that will have muddled her access to her own clarity. Fragile will emerge clear, in a great light, shining like a diamond, that will be the novel's point.

Fragile will emerge lit, like a gem in the lamp light . . . there is suddenly something I am reminded of, to do with burning coals.

Yeats? Lawrence? Shelley? I think it was Shelley. Burning coals burning coals burning coals . . . perhaps it was Coleridge, perhaps it was Keats. Shelley, I think. But one thing's for sure, Fragile is a subject, woven into her narrative, existing within her narrative frame. Don't get lyrical, Fragile.

She will use language sparingly. She will be subject to light and dark. Nothing of Derek about Fragile, she will be lit, softly spoken, with an id like a blade. Sure, absolutely sure, at some level, with little bursts of light and the ability to pitch into darkness. Somewhere, somehow, for some reason, she'll walk the burning coals. She'll be a dazzle in a dimly lit interior, an angel down a mine. Such vision as the world has barely seen, the clear view, the absolutely penetrating gaze.

I have been putting Fragile together gradually, over time. What is she made of? Trivial things, such as the afternoon I went to the shop where they have bare floorboards and a curving mirror, and Tchaikovsky's ballet suite on a ghetto blaster. They had a collection of bomber jackets with some limp little light silk blouses in toning colours: I wore dark charcoal with a sliver of grey; green with auburn; coral with blue. Then bought all of them and wore them practically never. That afternoon the girl who was so good at colours said, 'You know, you need a darker lipstick: here, this one'd suit you.' She went to her bag and slid out Rose Nature, in a smart black container with gold around the rim. She pushed it up and held it next to my face. The tones of my two silks fell into a new relation, and I went off to Lancôme and bought Rose Nature, which always reminds me now, when I push it up and touch my mouth with it, of _The Nutcracker Suite_, bare floorboards and emerald green silk.

What has that got to do with Fragile?

Nothing. It had to do with rebuilding me, in a particular way, with a particular care and a particular emphasis, so as to leave Fragile free of me. It had to do with writing *The Dark Heart of the Rose*. Nothing to do with the way Marianne and I did everything together, nothing to do with the way we dressed the same, spoke the same, thought the same, felt the same, saw the same: so that, at the penultimate moment, when everything could have been just about to come right, Marianne rebelled and stalked out on me. I was left — my work having been abandoned just when I needed it to be rounded, teased finally into shape, replete, complete — bereft, abandoned, with the traces of Marianne's last gesture all piled up in my heart: her sticks of charcoal; her bottle of asprins; her paper spread across the floor, right up to the edges of the walls; her knife. For a very long time I was determined that that was the end of *Marianne's Monster*, but Marianne would not let her own ghost rest. She haunted everyone. 'I don't like it,' said my most cherished reader. 'I thought, no I don't like this one at all.' 'I've read up to page two hundred and nineteen', said my singer friend, a year later: 'Can you send me the rest?' 'That's it,' I said. 'That's the end.' 'No!' he said. It was so badly in need of an ending, he felt, that he suggested a murder. Certainly a body ought to be found. But don't you see, I protested, that's the dilemma. That's the tension. Marianne is a body. That's what she is. She can't get out of her skin, don't you see? He thought about it. 'I think it would be better if she found an actual dead body,' he persisted. 'Don't you? I mean, you know, clearer.'

The whole wretched thing would have to be extended: I extended it. I went to Paris and wrote Marianne in Paris. I drank my brains out and wrote about Marianne going mad. I sent her up to an empty seaside town in winter to find the aforementioned body on the beach. I called this section 'Marianne on the Rocks'. It *ought* to have fitted. In section one of the book, Marianne is a child, abandoned by her father who goes missing, contending with her mother's new lover, trying to make sense of the missing link. In section two we trace the father to Paris, where he is living on the edge, a desperate figure, tortured, perhaps, by masculinity and its demands, trapped within himself, fighting to get out. Or back. His overcoat plays quite a large part in the novel, it is the bit of him everyone notices, the bit of him everyone remembers: his hugeness, his roughness, the flurry of something beating behind him as he comes and goes. Everyone's favourite section of the book is when he travels back to England and I take him to an empty seaside town on the East coast. The light is closed down for the winter, but the amusement arcades are still open, the sticks of rock are out there in the cold, displayed like organ pipes in their serried ranks; the buckets and spades, the plastic monster men are all strung out in tiers against the skyline. If I sent Marianne to the coast — to the edge of the world — to find his body, if I took her back, at the end of section three, to the scene where he is last sighted, that would be fitting, wouldn't it? Wouldn't that make the curve I wanted to make, the central line of the novel, the basic shape?

For some reason, it didn't really work. I described this new scene to one of my Faithful Readers. I'd given it such a good title: 'Marianne on the Rocks'. 'That's awful,' came the response. 'Too obvious.' I deleted it.

WHAT THE BLOODY HELL AM I GOING TO DO WITH HER THEN? I kept asking. If she can't just sort of hint that she's about to do herself in at the end, then what. . . 'Oh, is _that_ what she's doing on page two hundred and nine,' he said. 'Of course,' I insisted. 'It's symbolic. Don't you get it?' 'Er, no,' he said blankly. 'Why?' 'Why what?' 'Why does she have to commit suicide? Are you sure that's wise?' 'Look I just want her to DIE. O.K.?' Head-shaking. Feet-shuffling. 'I just don't see why.'

'What happened to the new bit, anyway?' 'No go,' I said. 'She did a thorough search of the beach, but she couldn't find anything.' 'Look, can't you just give yourself a break from it for a while?'

I couldn't get free, you see, and nor could she. Are you beginning to get the picture? That's where the drawing came in. I got there in the end, well, in as much as any of us can ever say that we got there in the end. I got free. But this is how I had to do it: I exchanged pain for pain. With a stick of charcoal between my fingers, I got free. Now Fragile is a burst of light on the threshhold of my imagination and somewhere in Fragile's world there are burning coals. In the interim, in the undergrowth, in 'the drawing,' there is one hell of a struggle, some intense despair, a lot of disorientation, and a little glow of pleasure: Molly, a model, a baby and me, all alive in Molly's kitchen one afternoon in the dark glow of dusk-coming, all working together in our own different ways, with mince pies halfway through and the baby playing at the model's feet and the model looking down and saying 'What pink little hands': Christmas. Nothing of Fragile yet, then, but a miracle of sorts, a nativity. It was coming, I knew it was; it was coming.

Nativity

Glancing back over this to see if it has any coherence at all, I find I have actually drawn a neat curve: what I am aiming at is a line which will get you from Egon Schiele, retrospectively back through Marianne and on, through the life drawing, to Fragile. I'll return to Egon Schiele in a minute.

Looking back now, it seems astonishing to me that for so long I could only see line. I literally could not see mass, not really. I hated tone. You practised getting tone with bottles and apples. Molly explained about light: it falls diagonally. Look — if you see it falling across that apple, you can see that it falls like water. Dark sort of tucks in. And then, on the human form, you can see how it tucks in round things like knees and ankles. Shoulder blades are always light; stomachs are usually light. But then look: just under the calf muscle, it's all in shadow.

This is rudimentary, of course. But you would be absolutely amazed how long it takes you to see it. I mean, to really take in the impact of planes and relations in this way. Same with foreshortening. At the beginning, you draw what you know. You know that when the model has one leg crossed over another, both legs are of equal length, so you draw huge expanses of thigh when you can actually only see a couple of inches. You learn to hold your pencil out and squint, to measure how little you can actually see, and how much.

I took life-drawing classes, as well as my lessons with Molly. The first time I drew a male model I panicked. He stood in a corner of the room, away from the clatter of easels, in an ochre jersey, his legs naked, waiting. He had floppy blond hair and an artificial tan; he was like a bronze statue, but slighter, lighter, more fleet. I was shaking, as I rigged up my easel, got out my charcoal. I thought life models were women. Nobody told me the model would be a man. He moved to centre-stage, peeled off the jersey. My muse stirred. Marianne stirred. I stirred. The model turned his back.

He bound both wrists with twine, held his arms outstretched. The pull of the twine taxed the muscles in his forearms, upper arms, shoulders; made a good line. That piece of twine gave him balance, gave him proportion; held his back, his shoulders, his thighs, his calves, his arms, his head, all in relation: in a beautiful figure of related lines.

I made one mark, just one. My charcoal was red hot; hard. I stood back, afraid of what I might draw, afraid of what I might see. Afraid of what I might do.

When he turned, and I saw his chest, his hips, his stomach, his penis nestling quietly, at rest while he stood erect, on display. I saw my muse sleeping. I saw the boyishness of my muse at rest, and the exact proportions of the body of my muse as he lay asleep: same shoulders, same chest, same thighs, same cock, same knees, same shins, same eyes. Same mouth.

Marianne, outraged at my audacity, observed me from the threshhold of my imagination: threatened me with teasing her, with taunting her, with bad mothering, with neglect. Marianne, pitifully dressed for a night out on the town, in her satin skirt, her dyed hair, her high heels, knowing everything except how to get me to get her to fuck, raged and raged as she stood in the doorway, gazing with fury at that man, and then she cried.

She crumpled up, she cried. She cried hot tears of frustration, she cried a river of rage. She was beside herself and could not stand up, she clawed at the door jamb for support; she began to look ridiculous in her seductive outfit, her dyed hair. She said a word I had let her say in section one of *Marianne's Monster*, when she was much smaller, just a little girl: a word she had uttered in the night, disturbed in her sleep by the vibration of her mother's love-making. She said, 'Mummy. . .'

I couldn't draw. When the model caught my eye and offered me the merest hint of a wink, his eyes lit up, his mouth relaxed, I saw the face of my muse in him. I forced myself to lift my charcoal: I made one more, tentative mark. Marianne howled.

I wanted that model. I wanted to tear off my clothes and get up onto that podium, and fuck him right there and then in front of the whole class. Could not, of course. Shelved that desire, as I got on with measuring, making marks, measuring, making marks. Looking, touching, looking.

Marianne had no such outlet for her passion, no such diversion, no such way of evading her desire. I think it was from that day on that I knew I had nowhere near finished writing the novel. I think it dates from that first day in the life-drawing class: my realization that I had barely begun to invent the real Marianne.

She could not agree to be shelved; I had to be.

'It's like choosing words,' I said. 'It's all about seeing and selecting. The whole story is always there: heart, lungs, knee joints, two equal-sized thighs, breasts, hair, eyes, haunches . . . but which bits do you want the reader to see.'

There are two schools of thought on the question of the model. One school sees the model as a sack of cement. In my class we had a new model, posed on a construction made out of wooden boxes, arranged across it were various different kinds of drapery; there was a bucket positioned at his side. 'I can't do this', I said. 'I don't like the drapery, I can't get the corners right on the boxes and I just don't like that bucket.' 'It's to give you a chance to get different textures,' said the teacher. 'I don't want different textures,' I said, 'I want psychological states.' The next week he brought in a book about Matisse. 'You see,' he said, 'Sometimes his arms and legs were unusual shapes, too. It's about perspective. About _how_ you want to show the figure.'

'Psychological states', mused Molly. 'Yes! I see what you mean. Maybe you've just got the wrong model. How's the writing going, by the way?' 'From bad to worse', I said. 'In fact, it's stopped.' 'Hm', said Molly. 'You know that model we had the first time,' I said to the Monday-morning teacher, 'the one who posed with bits of twine. . .' 'Oh, you mean Jake.' 'Yes: are we going to have him again?' 'People didn't like him much,' replied the teacher. 'They thought he was a bit . . . you know, all a bit much.' 'Isn't he coming back then?' 'I don't think so.'

After the break that day we did quick poses: fifty seconds, then the model moved. And so on and so on. I did six poses all on one page, it looked like a cartoon. 'I don't understand it,' said the teacher, bemused. 'You can only do it fast. Why can't you do it slow? It's mad.' 'Because if the model's moving, I can move,' I explained. 'If the model's lying there like a lump of concrete for an hour, I just sort of atrophy.' 'Mad. . .' he went away muttering. He went to his office and didn't come out for another forty minutes. All that time I worked at the bucket and couldn't get an ounce of life out of it, while everyone else sat placidly at their easels, rubbing away. Light, dark, light, dark, cross-hatching here, foreshortening there. At the end we looked at one another's. The one I liked the best had illicit trickles of cadmium to indicate the dark — or was it the light — tones. Mine looked like a piqued ventriloquist's dummy, his bucket propped at his side like a transvestite's handbag. The following Monday I missed the class: I had a sore throat.

Molly said, 'Look, I think I may have a new model. She's supposed to be the best in town, everyone adores drawing her. Are you interested? We could do it in my kitchen: it's warm there.'

Alessandra was one of those people, rare among women, who comes to life when nude. Just seated, legs crossed, hands on her knees, she had a lit quality, she looked like a painting by Botticelli; divested of her clothes she was simply divested of clutter. First of all I drew her crouched, towards the bottom of the page: small, delicate: 'it looks Chinese', she said. 'Look, let's start again,' said Molly, 'and do it big this time.' We had a break first, for mince pies and then she went to get the baby. She put him on the floor and he crawled straight over to Alessandra and touched her toes. It was nearly Christmas and this was holy. I cannot describe the drawing, but I knew that in the presence of this I had a responsibility. It was nothing to do, now, with drapery and buckets, it was to do with fecundity and new life, warmth and reverence and beauty.

I tried to go slowly. 'Keep the whole thing in mind,' said Molly, 'try to keep hold of the whole thing; don't forget the relationship between the bit you're doing and the rest.' I made a great breakthrough that day, a great discovery. I cannot even remember what it was, in detail, but it was a discovery about a relationship: something about the relationship between the curve of the shoulder and the mass of the haunch, or calf . . . I can't remember. I can't remember because I am not a visual artist. I can't remember which line, which plane, which mass. What I remember are the words. Alessandra looking down at the baby, playing at her feet, and saying, 'what pink little hands'. Molly saying, 'remember to keep the whole thing in mind.' I remember the mince pies, the way it got dark and the room began to sparkle with Christmas; the particular quality of the darkness when we got outside. If I filmed that afternoon, I would have French carols playing in the background. When I got out of that kitchen into the sparkling road, my green cardigan had darkened and deepened: it was the colour of a privet hedge in winter. My legs had definition, the way they do after swimming or dancing or sex. Concentration was all it was about. Paying new attention. Because what was there to be seen was about patience and grace and goodwill and light: that's life. That's drawing from life.

Perhaps that afternoon felt consecrated because I was germinating something other than the drawing during those two hours: perhaps it was a new seed of Fragile which consecrated that ground or perhaps I had touched the dark heart of Marianne, but from a safe place this time. Who knows. It was about relationships, as I have said already. Attention, communication, reciprocity, coming together. Somehow this was beginning to happen — as I knew it had to — outside the house of fiction. _Reculer pour mieux sauter_; returning home to leave home. . . Alessandra came back to my flat with me while I wrapped up a story I was about to take someone as a Christmas present. I wrapped it up in red paper. Alessandra said, 'I love red, but I hate maroon. I really hate maroon. I had a maroon phone, so I painted it blue. Now it doesn't ring properly.' After Christmas, she went to India. She sent me a dazzling turquoise card, with a picture of a beautiful bronze statue. 'I am getting thin and brown, just like the woman in the picture,' it read. The woman in the picture looked like her, though thinner and browner. I could see the potential for Alessandra — pale and lit, like a woman by Botticelli — to remodel herself into an Indian statue. 'Why doesn't she model for _Playboy_ and earn herself some money?' I asked Molly. 'Then she could spend her whole life going where she wanted'. 'I don't suppose she likes money,' said Molly. 'Too right on for that. What are we going to do now? Shall I get us another model?'

One Monday afternoon I came home from my class, fixed my drawings, washed up, ignored the ansaphone, and brought my drawing pad in here: into the room at the end of the house, with the view of the walled gardens and the books and the typewriter, my 'study'. I cleared the desk of papers, put my drawing pad across it, and made marks across the page dividing it into four, as for four related poses. Then I started to write into the space. I described a life-drawing session. I wrote about drawing a man. Then I think I either transcribed it onto the typewriter, making minor changes as I went along, or I put it into the third person. I can't remember which, or in which order. It was going to be the beginning. I just started. I marked that page with writing until it was marked all over, then I turned over, divided the next page into four and marked that page as well. I wrote about drawing and I wrote about desire. Something began to evolve; as I began to sketch it out, I realized I was drawing my first male model again, this time from memory; and something else was happening: as I worked, the muse entered. I worked on: touching; looking; watching the relationships, watching them closely. Paying minute attention. Drawing him to me. I drew a mate. I used what I had learned about drawing from life, and I wrote it. I made new marks in my writing; I was making new tones, planes and shapes.

I left it like that — I am remembering, now — I left it on the drawing pad for a few days, before typing it up. I feared it, the way I fear the marks I make when I draw: they show me how vulnerable I am, how little I know, how unpractised my eye really is, how shaky my hand, how limited my repertoire, how limited my knowledge.

But then after a few days, I picked it up and read it through and saw that something might . . . just might . . . . Perhaps it was a beginning. As I typed it up, I finalized the translation into my own medium. I painted it blue. I applied my blue pencil, I worked with facility over my marks, my lines; I am so much more practised at my toning, my marks are so much surer, in my own medium. Not that I hate maroon, of course. On the contrary: I am passionate about maroon, I am passionate about my drawing. But I am acutely aware of my lack of resources and knowledge, when I work in maroon.

Something moved. It was Marianne, stirring.

I worked those few pages in: sketching quickly at first, then working at my tones, trying to make my shape emerge; and as I worked towards completing it, I began to see the emerging shapes, and the relationships between them. I also started to see — just gradually, with a lot of tentativeness, and some fear — what was developing, out of my blocks of new marks.

Marianne moved. She murmured. Her eyelids flickered. She was alive. As I worked away quickly at these few pages, she stirred as from a little death. Marianne, while my back was turned, while I had been eating mince pies and drawing Alessandra, had picked up her broken shoe and her box of charcoal and she had gone off and done some drawing of her own. I came upon her again in the life-drawing class. She was quickened, she was focussed, she was working at relationships: she had her own male model, her own mass, line and marks (though my experience had informed and infiltrated hers, of course). When I had transposed those marks from my drawing pad onto my typewriter, I saw what I had done. Here was not a new novel, heroine or story. Here was my conclusion, in its own colours, to _Marianne's Monster_. Only when I discovered that I had not, after all, left her for dead, could I reach the point of knowing for certain that that novel — in its entirety, now, with a finished shape, a finished form — was alive.

I rang Brussels. 'I've got the ending for Marianne.' 'That's wonderful: how?' 'I've turned it round,' I said. 'She's her own artist. She draws from life. She draws a man, she looks at modelling, and discovers what it is, and then she can get married. She marries her model. She doesn't tell anyone. It's nobody's business but theirs. In the end she finds work and she finds privacy. She makes her own decision. And he doesn't have to go blind for it or be half her age. They work together. They come together. That's it. It's simple, really. I can't imagine why it took me so long to get there.'

'It sounds right,' he said. 'It is right.' I knew it was right because I had that feeling, at long last: that feeling you get in a plane, when the plane just lifts, ever so slightly with no noise, no fuss, just a little lift and, from being immersed in white fog, you are suddenly above the clouds. Flying at the highest possible altitude.

And Fragile? Sshh. Quiet. Hush. Go carefully for a while. Take care. Marianne must not be disturbed.

Life . . . (?)

After I had written the ending for *Marianne's Monster* (I have searched the house but I cannot find a copy of it anywhere. But I always do that with copies of things I feel this way about. There are not two Notre-Dames . . . you know what I mean), after I had written that new ending, I got an endorsement of it. They say you write the future: that if you invent something in fiction, it will happen. Well, there is a version of this: sometimes life endorses what you have done, it supplies a repeat, a refrain. Not an identical copy, but an event which feels significant, probably because of the status you have already given it in your original.

After I had given Marianne her male model, we found a model who had studied Egon Schiele. For two and a half hours of theatre, that man performed for me. We looked at Egon Schiele's self-portraits and selected some poses. He posed with stockings, with cloaks. He glanced at me as I coaxed his body into life on my page, he shone; his lines were warm and dark; I suddenly knew what to do about tone. I lifted my overall, used it to erase a mark. Molly, at my side, said, 'would you like a tissue, Sue?'

He moved; I moved. I shifted my weight from foot to foot, I stepped in and out of my shoes. There was incense, and music; the room was getting hotter; my charcoal began to feel warm and moist in my hand. I could feel my legs strengthening; my calf muscles, my thigh muscles going taut. I sketched more boldly, with bigger, broader lines. Molly said, 'Go on. . .' He broke the code which silences models. He said, 'when it works it's because there's a rapport between the artist and the model. . . . There are warming-up exercises you can do: massage, for instance, have you ever tried massage? It's about touch. Drawing from life is about touch.'

Molly and I decided that if it could be stockings one week it might be knives the next, we had better be careful. We fell outside onto the pavement with our sticks of charcoal, our wobbly easel, and confronted the weird light of an ordinary evening in the ordinary world (the way things sometimes look when you emerge from the cinema). We know the safety code: it is important not to be seen to be offering a stranger anything that might be interpreted as gratuitous provocation. You never know. Take care. Had we properly examined his credentials? If he had been proposing to get violent, he would probably have begun like this. How would you know? For women, there may not be such a thing as 'a bit of harmless porn'. This was not pornography, of course, it was something else. He was a sitter. We had engaged him and paid him, it was his job. But what kind of a defence would that be if you suddenly found yourself on the ground, at knife point? Schiele, of course, was imprisoned for his drawings; most of Schiele's work is regarded, even now, by some as obscene.

What was odd was that even when it was I who was doing the looking, even with the man as the object — of my gaze, my work; my desire — he was still the one who was in control.

Perhaps then I had discovered something about the controlling power of the object of desire; except that there is the inherent power of the male body which it is impossible to keep out of the equation, impossible to forget.

And who is the artist ever drawing, anyway: the model or herself? Himself? I had exposed myself to my model, by looking in the particular ways I had looked, seeing what I had seen, drawing what I had drawn, just as much as he had exposed himself to me. In taking this glimmer of a risk, I now know more about my own responses, more about my vision and my art.

We are looking for a model again. Models are transient, in these parts. They come, they go. Alessandra has been sighted, but seems not to be at her old address. Molly is investigating. 'We could always draw Egon Schiele again, of course,' she says. She gives me a sideways glance. She doubles up and peers backwards through her legs at me. As it were. But I am still pensive about it all. I am disappointed. There was more to do. It is a fact of life, and a pity, that it would be rarer for a male artist to feel the need to steer clear of a female model because of an obvious sexual attraction between them. Think how many great pictures would be lost to us, if that were the case. Think how few great pictures there would be in the world. (I am not, of course, claiming that I would ever have made a great drawing. But that's not the point). How would Schiele have fared? Degas; Picasso; Cézanne; Matisse. . . All I am saying is that it's a pity. That's all.

No I am not, I am making a link between sex and fear. Sex and death. Sex and violence? Somewhere tucked in darkly in the interstices of Marianne's story this connection lurked. It had been driving me crazy, throughout the writing of *Marianne's Monster*. I couldn't cope with it: it was a riddle without an answer. I couldn't see where it was coming from, or how it really related to Marianne's story — or what to do with it. Marianne's monster.

Sex and death. I drove myself into the ground on this one, I drove myself into maroon. When I saved Marianne from the terrible clutches of her own knife, on page two hundred and nine, I did so, eventually, by giving her a different ending altogether: one that allowed her a direct sexual response. Perhaps, prior to this, it was my *failure* to let her expose herself that had driven her to violence, madness, despair.

So that had answered one question. And perhaps my own exposure to the model, my reversal of roles so that I copied the *artist*, thereby exposing myself to the model's invitations, was the endorsement I needed to recognize what I had learned earlier, by drawing my first male nude: that I needed to see myself looking, to know that I was prepared to really see, before I could realize my own creation.

That other question — of the link between sex and violence — remains unanswered. As a sexually available woman, there is always the possibility that I could be violated, mutilated, maimed. But I could also touch my own death, without being abused. Of course. It was the illusion that this mystery could be solved that was the problem. The illusion that it could all somehow be solved: is that, perhaps, Marianne's monster? Certainly, Fragile who is frailer, more vulnerable and more patient, who takes life as it comes, is not looking for any solutions. All Fragile is seeking is the chance to test out the sound of her own voice. When in doubt, Fragile takes a different route: she sings.

Zutique

For a long time, I thought that what I was taking you towards, in this piece of writing, was the unexpurgated text of _The Dark Heart of the Rose_ and that in writing the earlier piece I would get myself back to the beginning, into the dark heart of my connection with my muse. I stripped something away, in that work, and I tried to push myself on into something new. I thought the heart of the problem was the difficulty of drawing on the self, which must nevertheless be shelved. I thought I was solving it, by writing fiction-as-biography. It wasn't autobiography, just a biography drawing on myself. A version — some of the bare bones. I stripped something away, uncovered a layer, and then sketched it back in: in new colours, this time, blue, maroon, rose. I looked in a mirror of my own making and saw myself all written backwards: a neatly expurgated child.

There was something at the heart of that process, though, which _The Dark Heart of the Rose_ itself could not reveal: a desire for something more grown-up, more passionate than I could inscribe. That piece of writing was like a sliver of light glancing on the threshhold between the last novel and the next, it sang out with a desire to consecrate something I had not yet arrived at, something I still had not yet understood.

Back in the park, I found Molly and the baby. And the Husband. All three, sitting equidistantly in a neat triangle. No trace of Frog. The Husband remarked that I looked very pretty in my colour-coordinated purple and yellow (I had changed into my cacophony-of-flowers skirt for the park). The baby looked up at me as if to say, 'Look, I'm not entirely sure I want you here *now*', for all the world like a man thirty years his senior. 'Hi! Fancy seeing you here!' exclaimed Molly. I was a bit careful, just in case there was any complicated reason why it should be such a surprise to see me. You never know, when you suddenly come upon a tableau like that with no warning.

It felt, then, as if *this* piece of writing (the one you are reading) had worked itself through something. Somehow, I had put an acceptable shape back in place, after all this tipping coins in the grass and Frog nearly getting lost. I have got the baby sitting upright between his parents: no more flipping up-side down, no more acrobatics; we can all get back into our patterns and be private. Although I wasn't thinking any of this, as I shuffled the pages of *The Dark Heart of the Rose* over a tepid capuccino. I was trying to work out why I had begun by intending to present and elucidate *The Dark Heart of the Rose* but ended by doing this — what I have done over the last forty or so pages — instead.

'Sue!' Molly's face appeared, somehow framed by a tree, like something out of *A Midsummer Night's Dream*. I had my brain programmed for quick-select, so I swiftly registered her blue shirt and maroon trousers, while the back of my mind grappled with trying to interpret the expression on her face and make sense of the fact that she had worked herself loose from her tableau. 'Sorry not to have been able to talk properly,' she said. 'I'll ring you in the week about getting a model. Yes?' 'Fine', I said. I was still having trouble with the idea of her sudden exile. I was trying to visualize the baby, the Husband and a gap for Molly. I knew the baby wouldn't put up with that for long. She smiled. I stared. It occurred to me that I should perhaps explain my blankness of mind. 'I've got all this new writing,' I said. 'The drawing's got in.' This would have been a great deal too cryptic for even the most practised interpreter, but it was no problem at all for Molly. 'Great!' she said. 'I'm really looking forward to seeing it. Must go!' I was left staring at a tree. My capuccino was cold and there were four people in fierce-looking biker jackets at the next table, all sweetly eating ice-lollies and staring at me the way I had stared at Molly. I flipped back into quick-select and continued with the business of combing _The Dark Heart of the Rose_ for the sections which seemed to relate most closely to the drawing. It was composed of tableaux, it struck me now, and running through it was a desire for consecration, and a need to conceal.

The Dark Heart of the Rose now feels like a tangible block of time, an interlude, without which my life could not have gone on — not in the way I needed it to. Marianne had bled me. Strange that I should have become quite so exhausted by a book that felt relatively easy (until that awful penultimate stage, when Marianne herself deserted me) to write. _The Dark Heart of the Rose_ was a desperate attempt to write myself back into the light. Marianne had plunged me in darkness: she drew on my nightmares, my deepest memories, my desire, and improvised on them ruthlessly. She flung herself at me in a rage for not making her sexual enough; she tore at me with her claws out for not being able to deliver her a happy ending. She fought and fought to extricate herself from the house of fiction I had made for her: she was a character and a half, that one, she was more than I could handle ... Yes, I know, I invented her. But there comes a point where they go from you: they take on their own personalities, just like the baby. They stare up at you from their place on the grass and _they_ decide. They talk, they walk, they have tantrums. I know how odd it sounds but I can't explain it. It's a mystery. You have some control — over the colour, the tone, the note, the light — but the rest is about crafting out of chaos. You chip away at it. You draw it, re-draw it; darken it; mould it and re-mould it. But as you do so, you penetrate deeper into this strange house you have made, and sometimes its ghosts reach out and touch you in the night. _The Dark Heart of the Rose_ — as I am just beginning to realize — was an attempt to occupy my own house again.

Drawing from life would mean drawing on the desire to go backwards, into a form of autobiography, and forwards, towards new birth. But that was only the beginning. One more thing struck me, as I read through *The Dark Heart of the Rose* again: my obvious determination not to relinquish the search for beauty; my desire to make something elegant, delicate, suggestive, discreet. Which may be incompatible with the need to expose. Who knows. I do not know the answer to that.

I have been looking, too, at my work on Egon Schiele, prior to going back yet again into Marianne's recalcitrant section three. I can see now that my study of him inscribes more than an attempt to work in a different medium: it was, perhaps, an attempt to catch *his* likeness, to learn courage and daring as well as colour, light, economy of line. And a desire, also, to work in the presence of genius, as Schiele himself had begun by taking ideas from Klimt.

Only one of the poems I wrote for Schiele stays with me and has any real resonance for me in thinking again about Marianne. It is the one I wrote last, after reading Rimbaud's poetry and thinking about Schiele's struggle with words. It is the nearest I got in my own medium to the work of Egon Schiele: through Rimbaud; my life drawing; Fragile's awakening; and the writing of *The Dark Heart of the Rose*. It is also the nearest I came, I now feel, to the work of reviving Marianne. It is not *quite* a poem, perhaps . . . but it stands as a fragment, a sketch, a tribute to the master.

And to that elusive, vital other: the muse.

Study for First Encounter
    her eyes
her brutal softness
her difficult flesh

her mouth like a bruise
fingers like fledglings
the tilt of the head

    her hair
straggling under her hat
her voice the gentle tap
of a leaf on the pane greening
our secret with late light
I am painting her *zutique*

Susan Sellers

Writing New Fictions

I asked some of my male friends what they would be interested in reading about in a book on women's fiction. Sexuality? Gender differences? Women's perception of men? Not a bit of it. Two things interested them. How do you find the courage to begin and to continue, and where do you find the time. Perhaps writing cuts through the sexual divide more penetratingly (?) than we know.

One of the best pieces of advice I have ever read on starting to write is an exercise by Nicky Edwards on time wasting.* Make a list of the various avoidance activities you engage in as a way of postponing writing, she suggests, then total up your score. One mark for minor distractions like reading the dictionary, two marks for fidgeting, three for major distractions such as spring-cleaning your desk, and so on. What I like about this exercise is its assumption that these displacement activities are normal. Make a cup of coffee, hoover the floor, stare blankly at your page: then write.

Writing entails risk, and the risk permeates many levels. There is risk in deciding to spend time writing and risk in committing yourself to paper. There is risk in allowing others to read what you have written. Perhaps the secret is not to be too pragmatic. When it comes to writing it doesn't pay to be too far-sighted. 'Live in day-tight compartments' Dale Carnegie, the worry-god, advises. If you think too much you'll paralyse yourself with fear. Get your writing down. Begin anywhere. And let the activity's own momentum carry you forward. Once you're working, once the writing is up and running, you'll become immersed in the problems that confront you. You'll forget about the fear that prevented you from starting. And you'll find the time. Very few writers work in ideal conditions. And those who have unlimited time at their disposal may even find this a handicap.

* 'A Ten-Minute Exercise on Time Wasting', in *Taking Reality by Surprise: Writing for Pleasure and Publication*, Susan Sellers ed., The Women's Press, 1991, pp 2–3.

Writing is not like learning to drive a car. You don't need to read the whole of the highway code before you start. In fact, you'll probably end up a bad writer if you do. You'll discover how to change gear, when to attempt a hill start or reverse around a corner as the need arises. The important thing is to begin.

Writing an Image

Every writer begins each new piece of writing from a different place. With some writers this might be a story, for others a character that intrigues or haunts them.* For the piece of writing I want to discuss here the starting point was an image.

Some years ago I attended a conference on women's learning at the University of Amsterdam. A board or cube representing the game of noughts and crosses hung in each of the conference locations. At the final plenary the organizers displayed the games at the front of the lecture hall. It was a strange sight, these Mondrian-like assemblies of colour and shape. A number of women were surprised to see them. They did not remember having noticed them, or recollected only now how one had hung beside or in front of them during a debate on childcare or women's rights. As the discussion developed to include the conference as a whole, the game became a symbol representing what each woman had experienced and wanted to express. The conjunctions of squares and circles fed into the debate, illustrating a remark about segregation or informing a heated exchange on women's writing. As I sat on the train home, I found myself doodling the game on my notepad. For me the conference had raised questions about women's differences, the discrepancies between the

* This is a point discussed in detail in 'Beginning to Write' in *Delighting the Heart: A Notebook by Women Writers*, Susan Sellers ed., The Women's Press, 1989, pp. 53–88.

images with which women are confronted and the complicated reality of our lives. The noughts and crosses grid
reminded me of the description of the text as a weave. The X,
turned on its side, became that other kind of cross (+) which,
joined to a nought, forms the women's sign (♀). Suddenly
the symbol embodied what had emerged as the conference's
theme. Through the telling of other stories, the standard
image of woman had been split open and redrawn in a new
weave.

The phrase 'time is a great healer' seems particularly
apposite when it comes to writing. I don't know how other
writers react, but for me there is a definite pattern. First there
is the exhiliration of finishing, the great surge of excitement
and release that comes from having written at all. You close
your folder, convinced that what you have created is full of
resonance and meaning, that this time you have succeeded in
producing a piece where the intention matches the effect. You
pour yourself a drink and spend the rest of the day basking in
a self-satisfied glow. Then you reread it. And despair sets in.
You tear the piece to smithereens and vow never to write
anything again. Versions of these two extremes permeate the
writing for an undetermined period of time. Depending on
how much of yourself you have invested, it might be years
before you can read it with equanimity. It's a little like
looking at old photographs. You can smile indulgently at
those sixties flares as a testament to a bygone you, but that
jacket you were seduced into buying and photographed in last
summer is another story. The novel I discuss here I have
chosen for precisely this reason. Written in my twenties, it is
the only completed piece of unpublished fiction I feel I can
consider with anything like objectivity. The notion of critical
distance is always loaded — especially when it is your own
writing you are analyzing — yet this early novel at least has
the advantage of producing a range of emotions and reactions.

In my early twenties I spent three years in Paris where I
became acquainted with a wealthy English couple. The living
room of their flat was divided into two by an aquarium. I was
fascinated by this underwater world, which had its own

modus operandi, its own laws, and which yet depended for its survival on a universe beyond its own. The aquarium was at once visually arresting and expressed a feeling I had at the time that we all construct a semblance of order, which is both precarious and safe. Like the noughts and crosses boards at the Amsterdam conference, the aquarium functioned as a resonant image for my life in Paris. With hindsight I realize it offered two vital ingredients for writing. Its movements and colours generated intrigue and the necessary desire, while the various ways in which it could be interpreted gave shape and cohesion to what I wrote. Beginning a work of fiction often feels like embarking on a journey into the unknown, and this anchoring point, whatever it might be, can provide a crucial landmark.

An image on its own, however potent it may be, does not in itself produce good narrative. I returned from Paris with a number of insights and ideas I felt it would be interesting to explore in writing. The aquarium reappeared in these drafts almost without my noticing, lending atmosphere to a room or presenting an object for my heroine to focus on while I examined her state of mind. In this extract for example, my protagonist, Melanie, contemplates her reflection in the glass side of the aquarium.

> The silent weaving of the fish threw long, trailing shadows that flickered through the reflection of her face and hair. She was Ophelia, sinking to her watery grave. . . . She turned the light in the aquarium on.
>
> Caught, as if transfixed for a second by the sudden illumination, everything inside the aquarium stopped. Melanie's image dissolved with the glare, and she found herself staring into the dark eye of a pirana, the tail of an angel fish flapping wildly in its mouth.

This rather prosaic use of the aquarium reiterates a number of elements already introduced into the narrative. In an early section for example, the schoolgirl Melanie is invited to a party. She escapes her parents' interrogations by locking herself in the bathroom. Relaxing in her bath, she invents an image of herself at the party as seductive, sexy, worldly-wise.

Her reverie is abruptly halted by her mother's knocking and anxious 'Is everything all right, dear?'. Closing her eyes, Melanie dreams she is Ophelia, swept by the swift current of the river to her death.

Increasingly, as the writing progressed and began to gener-ate possibilities and directions of its own, the image of an aquarium acquired its own life and had an impact on the narrative. In this next extract for example, Melanie's adoles-cent confusion as to which of the prefabricated roles for women she should adopt is figured in a dream sequence in which the aquarium image connects with one of a television. Melanie imagines she smashes her way through the television screen to enter its world as a contestant in a game show. The compère hands her a set of keys and she chooses one in the shape of a goldfish. She is directed to a series of boxes labelled with a number and question mark — and the predict-able happens. As Melanie uses the key to open the box, water floods out.

> The compère tried to close the door of the box — but it was too late.
>
> Water gushed onto the floor, tangling camera cables, knocking over flower vases and microphones. Panic-stricken, the audience rushed to the exits — only to discover that a safety-locking device had sealed all the doors.
>
> Water poured into the auditorium, drenching chairs and studio equipment, drowning hastily discarded programmes and items of clothing. The audience pushed and shoved and jostled each other in a last-ditch attempt to escape. The water was almost up to Melanie's shoulders. Somewhere in the auditorium, a woman began to scream.
>
> Suddenly, there was a lightening crash.
>
> The water had fused all the lights.
>
> The entire studio was plunged into darkness.

The references to an aquarium aided the organization and illustration of Melanie's story. In the passages cited so far, it offered a rich source of meanings and possibilities which, like the noughts and crosses games at the Amsterdam conference, also functioned as a means of structuring the narrative, either through repetition or, as in the case of the television dream game, variation. But these extracts presuppose the writer's conscious intention. Other scenes in the novel revealed only retrospectively how they might have been suggested by — and might contribute to — the central motif. In a sequence near the close of the narrative, for instance, Melanie matches the various personae she has tried out for herself in Paris against her parents' expectations of who she will be. The scene occurs at a turning point as Melanie, anxious to rid herself of the grief she feels at the break-up of a love affair and regain control of her life, decides to become self reliant. In a fantasized return to her childhood home, Melanie's aggressive new identity appears irrelevant as a glass wall divides her from her past. Like the world of the aquarium, the universe of home is beyond her reach.

As Melanie walked along the tarmacked road looking for the familiar privet hedge and black gate, she caught sight of a board on the wall of the garage her parents shared with their next door neighbours.

VISITS DAILY
ADMISSION £1

She pushed open the front garden gate, and stopped in surprise.

The cracked flag-stone path, the overgrown grass, her mother's flowerbeds had all disappeared, and a gleaming white ticket office stood incongruously in their place.

Melanie peered through the window at the front of the ticket office, and saw her father counting a pile of coins.

She knocked on the window.

One?, her father asked her, and tore a ticket from a roll. . . .

Mechanically, without so much as a glance at her daughter, Melanie's mother clipped her ticket and opened the front door.

Stepping into the carpeted hallway, Melanie saw a line of arrows indicating that she was to begin her tour in the lounge.

The room in which she had so often sat, with its Victorian

tiled fireplace, its lace curtains, its bowls of _pot pourri_, was exactly as Melanie remembered it, except that a glass wall, designed to protect the room from its daily procession of visitors, screened her from the past.

Melanie attends art school in Paris and her work echoes her different resolutions. The release that comes from accepting multiplicity is figured in her painting of the sea. Her approach contrasts with her previous obsession for control, and her painting is the antithesis of the closed world of the aquarium.

> Melanie dipped her brush in emerald and ivory and aqua-marine and painted swirls of sea across her canvas.
> She closed her eyes, and let her feelings about the sea dictate her painting.
> She wanted to paint the salty taste of the sea in her mouth, the sharp sting of it in her eyes.
> She wanted to paint its sound as it lapped the sides of their boat . . . the cold rush of the waves against her skin.

The water's gradual transition from an almost pedestrian device to a potent source of language, imagery and meaning suggested that it would feature in the novel's ending. The references to it required a final account, and Melanie's realization that identity is fluid made its inclusion apposite. This correlation between my initial interest in the aquarium and its increasingly prominent role within the narrative highlights the complex interaction between the writer's conscious intention and writing's own impact on the process of composition. I may not have planned to describe my heroine painting the sea, but its relation to the central image meant any other subject — a bowl of fruit, a vase of flowers, a single rose — felt discordant and without the layers of meaning water had by now acquired. Try as I might, I kept returning to water (was it by chance, I wonder, that one of the colours Melanie squeezes onto her palette is _aquamarine_?). The image of an aquarium profoundly influenced the development and organization of my fiction, although its contribution was not without constraint.

Writing a Theme

Should you begin fiction with a story or a desire to write about an issue or theme? One of the hardest lessons to learn when writing about writing is that whatever rule you painstakingly devise is certain to be disproved by countless writers working in exactly the opposite way. All you can do is be specific, tell how it was for a particular project and hope that this will shed light on how, in this instance, the writing was achieved. In addition to my fascination with the aquarium, I returned from Paris with a number of insights and ideas about how women negotiate the question of identity. I was intrigued by the prospect of a female *bildungsroman* that would chart the complicated passage from girl to womanhood. In this early section for example, culminating in Melanie's decision to spend a year as an au pair in Paris, I try to evoke the fears and frustrated fantasies of an adolescent girl.

Her father had wanted a boy. When Melanie was born there was a china plate on her bedroom door with *Peter John* painted across it in blue letters. At school she had tried hard to make her father proud of her. . . . Now she had given up trying. She was going to leave home. . . .

At least it was easier now that she had decided not to go to University. She had to be careful though. She thought of a card player spreading a fan of cards on a green baize table. One false move and she would lose the game. She remembered a cousin who had taken a year off to work in a hospital before applying to medical school. She would do the same. A year abroad to improve her languages. She imagined a visiting card with her name on it, followed by an impressive list of languages: English, French, German, Italian, Japanese. She'd love to learn Japanese. She'd trim her hair into a neat bob and learn to sit cross-legged on the floor. She'd wear a deep blue silk kimono embroidered with flowers and hang sophisticated erotica on her walls. Still, Paris was her best bet. She'd find a job as an au pair and live in a *chambre de bonne*, her casement windows opening out over the roofs of Paris. '*Au pair*'. She rolled the syllables with an appropriately French accent. Not schoolgirl. Not daughter. Free agent.

The motivation for this sequence was partly auto-biographical, though the process of composition quickly generated possibilities that were much more interesting than actual facts. While my parents had decided on the name Peter John in case I turned out to be a boy, it was never the portent it is in the novel.

Melanie's decision to leave home is paralleled in the narrative by an abortive attempt to lose her virginity. Invited to a party to celebrate the end of school exams, Melanie follows a boy out into the garden. She has rehearsed the scene many times in her imagination, and is so intent on her own performance she is unable to accommodate the reality. It is cold outside and the garden railings press painfully into her back. She closes her eyes, endeavouring to piece together the remnants of her dream.

> But he was moving too quickly for her.
> She hadn't decided which part to play.
> Already his tongue was thrusting itself inside her mouth.
> She blocked out the scenario she had rehearsed (the flowers, the moonlight, the adoration in his eyes) and tried to concentrate.
> His hand was fumbling with the buttons oon her shirt.
> She felt herself becoming hard and aggressive and desirable (wasn't this the person he making love to?).

The scene sets a keynote for Melanie's quest to discover who she might be by modelling herself on the way others appear to perceive her. Her triumph in persuading her parents to let her go to Paris is accompanied by fantasies about the confident persona she will become. The fragility of this new identity is revealed as she prepares to say goodbye.

> Getting up that morning, Melanie had felt like a stranger in her own home. She had undergone a dramatic transformation during the night.
> For one thing, she was taller.
> And thinner.
> And more sophisticated.
> As she came downstairs, she stopped to look at the photographs of herself on the hall dresser. She had been an attractive child, she thought, as she went into the dining room.

Her father looked up at her from behind his paper and asked (for the hundredth time) was she sure she had everything? Her passport? Her ticket? Her timetable? He was making her feel like a little girl. No, she snapped at her mother, she did not want any scrambled egg. She didn't care whether her mother had cooked the eggs especially for her. She no longer liked scrambled egg. In fact she did not want any breakfast at all.

The clocks were not keeping proper time. Just a few minutes before, she had been getting ready in her room and there had been endless time, hours and hours before the taxi came. Then time had speeded up. She was gulping down a glass of juice, and suddenly the taxi was there. And now she had to say goodbye. Goodbye I love you, she wanted to say, don't forget me. But her mother was crying, and her father fussing with the driver about directions. . . . She ran, almost flung herself into the taxi and slammed the door shut behind her.

Come on, please hurry. . . .

At last she was on her way.

One aspect of identity that has always intrigued me is the component of fantasy in our vision of our lives. In *The Aquarium* I was interested in the way existing narratives — the stories our parents tell us, those we read or hear — interact with and influence our decisions about who to be. In this next extract Melanie, en route to France, has a number of scenarios running concurrently in her head. Her regression to childhood versions of herself once she has left the constraining securities of home highlights her incapacity to assume adult status.

What the passport controller did not know was that Melanie was a spy. Stowed in her suitcase, wrapped in the pink dress she had spent her final term's allowance on, were several reels of microfilm (images of herself in pink sipping *kir* in chic Parisian cafés intersected with those of the microfilm, Melanie almost lost the thread of her story; she wrestled with the dress. . .). She had been sent to London, she reminded herself, where she had successfully impersonated an eighteen year old schoolgirl, until an unlucky accident had almost blown her cover. Now, thanks to an opportune phonecall, she was off to Paris, her identity safe, to pose as an au pair.

The man leaning against the railings, apparently staring into the grey expanse of sea, was watching her. Perhaps he was a Home Office agent, or worked for Scotland Yard, though when he offered to buy her a drink and asked about her family, Melanie found herself telling a different story, how she was an orphan, returning to her native France after eleven years in an English school.

Gare du Nord. Terminus. Tout le monde descend.

As the train slowed to a halt, Melanie felt as if her new persona (the one she had put on that morning with her blue linen suit) was collapsing under her like a badly erected deckchair. The suit suddenly seemed wildly inappropriate. She was overdressed, she told herself as she collected her luggage, whatever would they think of her?

An important turning point occurs as Melanie, installed in Paris, navigates the bewildering maze of options that confronts women. Should she try for a prestigious career like her friend Isabelle, or marry like Christine? Her loneliness and indecision lure her into a classic trap. Asked what she wants from life, Melanie finds herself dreaming of joy: 'a leader, a companion, someone to show her the way'.

A premonition of the dangers of allowing another to dictate her life arises during a visit to the Impressionist gallery in the Tuileries. A series of images of women stare down at Melanie from the gallery walls, images that are echoed in the life-styles and attitudes of the women looking at the paintings. Melanie sketches some of the women, but the image that attracts her is Manet's portrait of Olympia.

Stop, look, you have painted me, it seemed to say, have created me from your desire, have made me white and the woman who is bringing me flowers black, have fastened this bow around my neck, this bangle round my wrist, pressed this scarlet flower behind my ear. I lie here in the pose you selected, as you ordained, unable to look at the woman you chose to accompany me, compelled to look at you.

Haunted by the charge, Melanie sketches other versions of Olympia — standing, walking, talking to her maid. But her drawings have no impact on Olympia's glare: her eyes remain angry, accusatory, full of reproach. That night, at a discothèque, the kaleidoscope of images Melanie has seen spins before her.

How did women decide which of these images was theirs?
Did women decide?
Would she?

And what would happen to all those other Melanies, she wondered, all those other versions of herself? Would they close inside one another like Russian dolls? Or would they, like a set of trick mirrors, continue to unfold on her, so that, when she looked, she would see other reflections, other images, grinning at her, mocking her, and have to slam the lid down tight?

Suddenly the whole idea of choosing seemed riduculous to her.

She was tired of thinking, tired of dancing alone.

She looked around for a partner.

Invited to dinner by her employer, Melanie makes a play for his young assistant — and falls in love. Her problems are over. She no longer needs to choose. Taking her cue from Philippe she has a ready-made identity. Philippe primes her in advance on who she shall be, what she shall wear, how she shall present herself to the world. Over time Melanie learns to read the signals of Philippe's desire, and schools her reactions to chime with his. She is safe, having abdicated   possibility for the secure tyranny of another's love.

There are various indications of the fragility of Melanie's new persona. Her fantasy of marriage to Philippe shatters as she imagines him spending Christmas with her parents.

As Melanie perfects the role of Philippe's dream girl, its strictures imprison them both. She becomes increasingly estranged from the real world of doubt and decision making, and retreats into fantasy. Philippe, initially gratified by Melanie's adulation, chafes against its impositions and rejects her. In this next extract, Melanie anxiously waits for Philippe to help her choose a dress for his office party, until the lateness of the hour and shop assistants' suspicious glances force her to her feet.

She began looking along the rails of clothes. An assistant was instantly at her side, pulling dress after dress off the padded hangers and holding them up for her approval. Did

Madame want red, did Madame want green, did Madame prefer a high neck or long sleeves?

But Madame didn't know, kept checking her watch, hoping, praying, willing Philippe to come.

Her watch ticked to half past.

In desperation, Melanie accepted the assistant's assurance that black was her colour, and hurried into the changing room, a pile of black clothes on her arm. She took a short black dress off its hanger, and held it up against her. She had to get a grip on herself. She was only trying on clothes after all.

But the dress was too tight, the next one too big, the third hung limply like a rag.

She tried on a fourth dress, then a fifth. Nothing fitted. Nothing was right. Without Philippe there to advise her, everything she tried on looked awful. Her reflection in the mirror was a disaster, she could never go to the party dressed like that. She tore off the dress and flung it on the heap of discarded clothing, fighting back the tears that were threatening to engulf her, mirror, dresses, changing room, in a sea of bitter despair.

The emphasis on physical appearance in this passage extends through the novel as Melanie's quest for identity is accompanied by her experimentation with clothes, make up and hair styles. This seemed both an interesting aspect of female psychology — as women we have unique social permission to cosmetically alter our external selves — and offered a fund of concrete images for the more abstract notion of identity. Perhaps, in answer to the question with which I began this section, it is this dramatization of ideas that is important. Good ideas are the life blood of fiction, yet it is the way these ideas are fleshed out and recounted that distinguishes the novel from other generic forms. Melanie's continual changing of clothes and hair styles were also sections I enjoyed writing, providing oases of pleasure amid the all too frequent battles of composition.

When Melanie discovers Philippe is having an affair, she takes refuge in a fantasy of tragic widowhood. Her anxious friends engineer introductions to other men, but she is unable to forget Philippe.

It was as if, when Philippe put his ring on her finger, he had drawn her inside a circle where only his influence held sway. It was like a game of grandmother's footsteps played on the other side of a mirror. As long as Philippe's gaze was upon her, Melanie lived, breathed, moved, but the second his back was turned to her, she was paralyzed, immobilized, a being cast to stone. The fact that Philippe had now abandoned her only increased the magnetic pull his hold exerted. She no longer had to deal with the reality of his presence, his unforeseen mood swings, his sudden changes of mind. Now that Philippe had left her, she could dispense with the unpredictable nature of his ego altogether, distilling his memory into the God of her imagination, directing her, giving her life, like his diamond forever.

This passage illustrates the curious generation that takes place in the course of writing. Earlier, while waiting for Philippe, Melanie had seen the advertisement 'diamonds are forever' in a jeweller's shop window, and Philippe's birthday gift of a diamond ring is engraved with the word 'forever'. The reiteration of the cliché deflates Melanie's ridiculous romanticism, and underscores how destructive such fantasies can be for women.

A third turning point occurs as Melanie, abandoning the role of tragic heroine, decides on a different tack. Disturbed by the sight of a blind man negotiating his way in the Paris underground, Melanie reassesses her position.

That night, as she sat at her dressing table, Melanie thought about the man on the train. An image of herself groping blindly through the darkness haunted her reflection in the glass. She picked up the torch her mother had given her in the event of a power failure and shone it at her face.

Haloed by the light, her reflection appeared disconnected from her, as if she were staring at herself through a kaleidoscope of mirrors. Christine, Isabelle, Emilie, Monsieur and Madame Robert — the glass threw back an echoing sea of faces that seemed now to betray her. She raised the torch to her forehead, and watched its beam reconnect her features, bringing back into focus the face she had all but forgotten, the face she had all but sacrificed in her eagerness to please.

From now on, she told herself, arranging the torch in her drawer, she would look to herself for guidance.

From now on she was going to take control.

Melanie's relinquishing of passivity and adoption of a more aggressively masculine stance is imaged in a parallel quest for knowledge. Scouring the encyclopedias in her employer's library, she searches for a blueprint that will translate the doubt and confusion she feels into irrefutable truth. Her desire for order is mirrored by the endeavour to organize her life according to a strict programme of self-advancement. She adopts a rigid daily routine that eventually affects even her art: 'She could no longer spread her paints haphazardly around her, experiment with form and colour, angle and line. . . . Her work became derivative, unimaginative, confined'.

Melanie's desire for order stifles not only her creativity but also her ability to form relationships. Her second affair is a reversal of the first as her attempted imposition of an identity on her partner forces his retreat. The phallic nature of Melanie's behaviour is underscored during a visit to that bastion of male privilege, the stock exchange. Listening to her guide's explanations of how investments are calculated, risks minimized and profits guaranteed, Melanie contemplates the frenetic activity of the brokers.

> Suddenly, she understood. It was a clockwork menagerie. A little boy's automated game. A magic picture show in which the self was not implicated and the other had no place, revolving to the dictates of a fraudulent monopoly, the ritualized misuse of power.

Finding a way to express Melanie's emergence from this classic masculine stance proved problematic. I tried a number of ideas, some of which are included in the narrative. Yet these episodes seemed insufficient; I felt I needed to effect the transition more dramatically. I spent weeks endeavouring to write my way through the block, and even considered abandoning the entire project. Then the unexpected happened. I wrote *The Aquarium* in a new house on the edge of a building site, and spent many frustrating hours forcing myself to concentrate above the noise of cement mixers and dumper trucks. For one onerous week I had workmen constructing a footpath and driveway directly outside my study window. I resorted to getting up earlier and earlier to avoid their calls of 'how's it going luv?'. Then one morning all was quiet. The footpath and driveway were completed. The workmen had moved on to the next plot of houses. I could return to my problematic narrative. Just as I was beginning to relax a workman appeared from nowhere. 'It's all right', he grinned through the window, 'I was only checking your manhole. You never know what might come up'. It struck me as a wonderfully apposite image, and an important lesson in writing. Even the worst scenarios produce their own solutions.

> The manhole cover clanged against the tarmac. A spear of light shot towards Melanie as she climbed the last of the metal rungs up the inside of the tunnel. She gave the cover a final push, manoeuvred it clear of the opening, and peered out over the rim.
> The shoes and ankles of passers-by clicked and tapped across the pavement.
> She thrust her head out of the opening, squeezing neck and shoulders up between the sides of the shaft. She pulled and twisted and wriggled her arms free, kicking and wrenching her legs through the narrow hole.

This rebirth is echoed in Melanie's decision to renounce her regime of self-promotion. Returning to Paris after a holiday by the sea, she reaches a different conclusion as to how to live her life.

> Back in Paris, Melanie abandoned her programme. She took down the time sheets she had pinned to her wall, put her grammar books back for reference on the shelf. She no longer wanted to master time, to carve her day into a precise schedule of component tasks with its illusion of progress and power. She wanted to inhabit time. . . . She wanted to sit on the cliffs and watch its changing colours, the red of sunset deepening to orange slowly fading to pink, as the light disappeared and the world flattened into itself and dissolved in the oncoming night.

The return to water imagery accompanies Melanie's realization that identity is fluid, an understanding represented in her painting of Notre-Dame. Earlier in the narrative, Melanie had watched an artist paint the cathedral, and the incident had prompted her to consider the relationship between perception and reality.

So which was the real Notre-Dame, she wondered, side-stepping a group of tourists posing against the backdrop of the cathedral, the artist's painting, the tourists' photograph, or the Notre-Dame she, Melanie, could see?

When Melanie looked at Notre-Dame, she saw sunlight reflected on stained glass windows and yellowing trees that reminded her of London, kicking trails of leaves across the park on her way home from school.

The artist saw angles and arches and flecks of white on a grey background, and a profit if he sold the painting.

(Was he ever tempted to paint the price in, Melanie wondered, instead of sticking it on a tag in the corner afterwards, for it was part of what he painted, part of what he saw after all?)

And the tourists looking at their photographs in Boston or Texas or Alabama, what did they see?

Melanie's own attempt to reproduce the scene is at first hampered by her knowledge that her viewpoint is a shifting one.

What was the relationship, then, she mused, adding a daub of yellow to her sky, between this painting and the one she would work on tomorrow, between her constantly changing vision and the real Notre-Dame? . . . . She thought of the magician her grandmother had taken her to see when she was little, a tall figure in a dark cape pulling rabbits out of hats and handkerchiefs and cabbages from behind his ears. She remembered how she had cried at the enormity of it all, and how her grandmother, trying to calm her, had told her we were the ones who created the illusion, connecting hat and handkerchief and hand in a logical sequence, we were the magicians.

She looked at her painting.

Her Notre-Dame.

As I retyped this last quotation, the correlation between the grandmother and Notre-Dame — literally 'Our Lady' — struck me. I began to imagine a skein of new scenes, and I have no doubt that were I to go back to the novel there would be some I would want to include. So writing is never finished. What we wrote yesterday is not (necessarily) what we would write today. Which seems the best reason for writing.

Writing a Story

A resonant image, a compelling theme, these are vital ingredients for fiction, yet the litmus test of narrative has to be its story. For many writers it may well be the story that emerges first. In *The Aquarium* it was the conjunction of an image with questions I had about women's identity that prompted me to write. Perhaps, in the end, it is this desire that is important. There may be writers who work from a sense of obligation, but for me desire has always been crucial in circumventing the crises of confidence that can otherwise prevent beginning. I don't know if the 'just one more cup of coffee' syndrome is gender specific; what I do know is that the fear is real.

Once I had written a number of cameo pieces I began to work on a story-line. Looking at the notes I made at the time I realize I had three main headings: 'role models', 'role stories' and 'language/naming'. Under each heading I had listed in random order a set of possible scenarios. Under 'role models' for example, there is a list of the different roles women assume together with suggestions as to how Melanie might meet such women. Each encounter provided the potential for a new twist to the plot.

An initial group of role models are the wives and mothers Melanie sees on her way to Paris.

> She took her note pad out of her bag, deciding to make a list
> of the things she wanted to do in Paris. But instead of the list
> she started drawing. An egg, then a frog. A man and woman.
> The man and woman were lovers (Melanie framed a giant
> heart around them) and very happy (she exaggerated their

smiles). In fact they were getting married (here her artistic
cravings ran away with her and she designed a massive
cake). She sketched tier upon tier of rosebuds and swirls,
culminating in an arch that curved like a prison door over the
newly wedded couple.

Then Melanie drew a knife.

(The group of women to her right finished the story of the
neighbour who was getting married and started on the couple
who owned the pub.)

The knife cut a chunk from the cake (she heard the words
'bastard' and 'tart'), then another chunk (here the women's
voices dropped to a whisper so that now all Melanie could
hear was the baby crying), and another chunk, until the cake
was riddled with missing pieces.

Melanie's friends in Paris similarly represent through their
dif-ferent choices a range of possible models. Again, I decided to image this relationship by having Melanie paint the
three women with whom she has formed the strongest bonds.
The painting pro-vided an unexpected opportunity to link the
issue of identity to my central motif, prefiguring Melanie's
discovery that identity is fluid which constitutes the novel's
ending. Having left a blank space on her canvas, Melanie
decides to add herself. Uncertain which colour to choose, she
mixes the red, yellow and blue she has used for her friends
and paints herself as a green mermaid.

The question of which model, which role to play, is also
developed through reference to the theatre. Melanie's employers are keen theatre-goers, and a visit to the theatre
prompts Melanie to remember her own appearance in a
school play. She recalls a dream she had the night before
the first performance in which she forgets her lines. Despite
protestations, she is forced onto the stage, and decides in
the dream that her only recourse is to invent her lines as she
goes. The memory shapes a second dream in which, standing alone on a stage with a spotlight upon her, she sum-
mons up her courage and sings out her name. As it rever-
berates around the auditorium the realization dawns on her:
'There were no words. No strings attached. She could play
any part she could invent'.

The stories we hear and tell ourselves similarly offered a rich source of narrative.

> When Melanie was little, frogs wore crowns and turned into Princes whenever they were kissed by golden haired Princesses who fell in love as easily as they fell asleep. Though the Princesses sometimes pricked their fingers on rusty spindles, though jealous spinsters tried to poison them and rival suitors cast them in evil spells, on the whole things turned out according to plan. The world had a fixed order, dreams followed a standard pattern, and predictions came true according to an inexorable reality that had been laid down at the start.
> You knew what your chances were.
> You knew what the stakes were.
> And (most important of all) you knew the price of failure.
> Either you found your frog and kissed him.
> Or you ate the poisoned apple.
> (Either way the outcome was pretty much the same.)
> Either you turned your frog into your Prince and were doomed to your happy-ever-after.
> Or you died.

As with other elements of the narrative, the reference to Sleeping Beauty recurred in unexpected ways. In this next extract a dream highlights the more sinister aspects of this romantic fairy story. The dream connects to Melanie's realization that love has transformed time into a seamless present and once again evokes the aquarium image.

> There was the now, full of memory and rehearsal, in which she relived every word, every gesture, of the previous meeting or planned the evening to come; the now in which everything else, people talking, people laughing, people going about their business, failed to have any meaning, seemed separated from her by a wall of glass. Then there was the now of being with Philippe; the now where time stood still, where each look, each kiss, became a moment containing the whole of time, eternal, suspended, like a bubble rising above the world, a unique rainbow paradise only the two of them inhabited.
> She lay asleep on a grass bank strewn with flowers.
> Though she was young, and very beautiful, she had been asleep for a hundred years.

On the final day of the hundredth year of sleep a frog appeared on the bank where she lay.

The frog saw Melanie and croaked and hopped until it had forced her wide awake.

Melanie opened her eyes and looked at the frog and knew her fairy tale of waiting had come true.

She stroked the frog then knelt down and kissed it.

No sooner had she done so than the frog turned into Philippe and a bubble burst scattering diamonds on the bank where the lovers lay.

Melanie nestled in her lover's arms, and watched a shoal of rainbow-coloured fish and heart-shaped lilies opening their petals in an aquatic ballet.

Suddenly, a shadow rose over Melanie and Melanie looked and recognized the shadow as her own. . . .

Its arms and legs and head flailed in a dozen different directions. . . .

At last, with a jerk, the shadow broke free.

Her shadow no longer belonged to her. . . .

Shadowless, she was doomed to wander the earth, with only a memory to haunt her now and then, as she opened a door or, gazing into a pool of water lilies, fancied she saw something stirring there, a question mark, an echo, of that other, unnamed still-born self, the ghost of lost possibility.

Naming, as an aspect of identity, is a contentious issue for women and formed the basis for a number of developments within the narrative. Towards the end of her affair with Philippe, Melanie visits the ancient Egyptian section of the Louvre. A body has been removed from one of the sarcophagi and exhibited in a glass case, and in this next extract Melanie imagines herself on display to visitors in a future space-age.

Would she mean as little to the silver-suited visitors of the future, she pondered, as this ancient Egyptian now meant to her? Did time always bury its sphinx-like secret, so that each new age, each generation, had to rediscover it afresh? She thought of all the wisdom stored in the ancient hieroglyphs, symbols which, if only she could read them, would tell the truth about the past. And once she knew about the past, once she had the key, then she would know about the present, could unravel the riddle of the Emperor, the eye, the two-headed monster and the fish, and make it make sense. . . .

Why did time always escape her. . . . In London she had spent her days dreaming towards an imaginary future, now all she could think about was her meeting with Philippe. She relived every moment of their first weeks together, the magic of it, of her, as Philippe loved her and suddenly she was transformed. Philippe had given her a name, and the name created her in a way her own name had never done.

Chérie.

When Philippe said her name, Melanie danced and span in a thousand pirouettes.

Ma chérie.

Language is a key component in the way we perceive ourselves, others and the world and gave rise to a number of episodes in the narrative. In this next extract for example, Melanie, committed to her programme of self-advancement, works on her French and discovers through the process of translation he innate unreliability of language.

Voler didn't only mean to steal.

Voler also meant to fly.

The pieces of Melanie's linguistic puzzle broke free from the order into which she had cast them. Words jigged and danced on the page before her, treacherously refusing to fit her meaning, defying her attempt to control. She blinked, and saw that behind what she had taken for the solid signs of meaning were winged birds of prey, awaiting the smallest chink in her armour to pounce.

She looked at her name.

Would that too betray her?

Were there other meanings hidden behind her name?

Meanings other than the ones she thought she knew?

Language is a crucial subject of feminist debate; whether we believe equality lies in neutering (humankind, chairperson) or are advocates of exploring the feminine, it is hard to deny the supremacy of masculine forms. This condition of language presented a means of dramatizing Melanie's (masculine) decision to promote herself at others' expense. Concluding that her difficulties in French are due to an inadequate grasp of its rules, she embarks on a thorough revision of French grammar. As her mastery increases, she assumes a position of command at the head of her sentence: relegating '*tu* and *il* and *elle* to their rightful places as the ordered subordinates of her all-powerful I'.

Language, as contemporary critics have shown, can also be employed against itself to undermine its own conventions and multiply the possibilities for meaning. This more radically feminine position is illustrated as Melanie translates between French, English and Spanish. Unable to find the words she needs to describe the frozen chickens in a local supermarket, she resorts to labelling them 'dead'.

> *Los polluelos estan muertos.*
> *Les poulets sont morts.*
> In French, in Spanish, her thought broke free from the automatic process thinking had become. In English, thoughts were already formed, already shaped and divided by the thinking that surrounded her, other people's thinking, the way society taught her to think. Pre-packed and frozen thinking, which prevented her from thinking, from seeing what she was seeing now.
> *Hundreds and hundreds of dead chickens.*
> In French, in Spanish, she had to work at her meanings, like an explorer she had to discover her words. And the words were different, changing the habitual meanings, giving them new possibilities, bringing them to life.

The correlation between language/naming and rebirth is present in the novel's ending, where the reconstitution of Melanie's name again evokes the aquarium image.

> She looked into the mirror.
> In her dream she saw an underwater world, full of sunlight and shadow and unfathomed depths. She pulled off her clothes, collected herself, and dived through the glass. . . .
> From the depths below, she heard a voice calling her, a voice that sounded both familiar and strange. . . .
> As she listened, the notes resolved themselves into a pattern she recognized.

> Mellllllanie

> Melanieeeeee

Melanie

Turning, she answered their call.

Writing a Character

Character, in the conventional sense, is mainly absent from *The Aquarium*. My protagonist has the function of filtering consciousness, distending and contracting, like Lewis Carroll's Alice, through a series of psychological states as her perceptions and fantasies alter. Absorbing and credible characters are nevertheless the mainstay of good fiction. A writing workshop I attended some years ago was insistent on this point. We spent weeks devising the biographies of imaginary characters. The exercises were useful and enjoyable, though as is often the case with writing exercises they had little direct impact on the work we finally produced.

A few rules do nonetheless apply when creating characters for fiction. Deciding on a first or third person perspective immediately imposes certain conditions on the writing. A first person narrative affects the presentation of other characters, who are mediated through the central 'I'. Third person narration, on the other hand, brings the author's relation to the fiction into focus. Happily the distinctions are not water tight and there are many interesting ways round the dilemmas. Julian Barnes' novel *Talking It Over* avoids the major difficulty of first person narrative by allowing each of his characters to 'talk it over' in their own voice. Emily Brontë's classic novel *Wuthering Heights* side-steps the problem of authorial knowledge by assigning the 'author' a role in the tale. Of course, the first and third person singulars are not the only possibilities, and there are a number of fictions that employ the second person ('you') as subject, or even the first and third person plurals.

One of the great debates of literature is whether or not women and men can write characters of the opposite sex. Jane

Austen's heroes are notoriously wooden, while D.H. Lawrence's men-obsessed women leave this woman wondering where his models came from. Although the question is circumvented in *The Aquarium* since all the characters are presented from my protagonist's viewpoint, the debate generally seems to me a red herring. Unless you are writing about experiences that can only be sex specific, I would suggest that the difficulties and solutions are roughly the same. Research, empathy and imagination are the crucial components of writing, and are as likely, as they are unlikely, to produce a convincing portrayal of, say, imprisonment. My insight as a woman might make it easier for me to imagine the effect of police innuendo on a woman prisoner, but the mental leap involved in writing about the ordeal would be the same for either sex.

Writing a Form

A male writer I know begins his novels with a structural outline that resembles a mathematical diagram. I am both envious and fearful of his prevision. I envy his evasion of those moments when the narrative grinds to a premature halt and you are left casting around for a way to set it going again. I wonder, though, what happens when the writing itself generates unexpected possibilities and new directions? Is the outline modified to accommodate them? Or are they tyrannously dismissed and the original blueprint adhered to? It's an interesting question and one which may well be gender specific. There have been recent moves in women's fiction towards a less controlled and more fluid form of writing it is left to the reader to organize and make sense of. I have sympathies with this position. After all, it is by imposing meaning that patriarchy has conspired to survive. But fluidity of form does not mean formlessness. I confess I have difficulties with those works of fiction where dis-order is synonymous with non-sense. Problems of comprehension can rob writing of its impact, hindering the identifications that propel us into other experiences. It is hard to empathize with Ophelia's plight if, as reader, you are painstakingly stringing together unpunctuated sentences or joining disparate scenes. In this sense, I believe the traditional pleasures of form should not be completely disregarded, since they may prompt us to transgress more as a result of the base-lines of known direction they provide. Like most people who write, I tend to look to the books I enjoy reading for my models. Although I'm not (necessarily) an advocate of conventional form, I feel there should be movement in fiction and, at the end, a sense that something has been answered or attained. The resolution may well be a negative one: the heroine may die, may lose lover, children, home, but I need to know, at the very least, *how* she arrived at her tragic end. Perhaps this desire says something else about the importance of form. Immersed in the minutiae of our lives, stories provide structures, models, insights — the expression and confirmation of our experience. Perhaps this is why fiction is so important to us. We turn to the novel for an outsider's view, requiring the novelist to sift through the complex data and communicate their understanding in dynamic and productive ways.

In *The Aquarium*, the form emerged through the telling of my protagonist's story. The various turning points demanded illustration and exploration, dividing the narrative into sections I decided should be of approximately equal length. This provided an overall frame, impelling me to prune some sections and expand others. In retrospect, I realize that those sections I wrote straight off contain fewest revisions and some of the best writing, while those I consciously had to develop include some of the more ingenious narrative twists.

A second formal principle derived from my decision that my protagonist would spend a year in Paris. It was an arbitrary choice, yet its potential underscoring of Melanie's journey of self-discovery was quickly apparent. Her endeavour to advance without others is set against the Parisian winter, while her rebirth into life coincides with the advent of spring.

One of the greatest hurdles in longer works is finding the confidence, energy and direction to continue. Here, an overall plan, however tentative and however much you alter it, can be an advantage. In _The Aquarium_, having some sense of how the narrative would develop was important, both in gauging the relevance and position of ideas as they emerged and because it offered a promise that I could — and therefore should — finish.

Beyond this overall guide, the form of each section developed in the course of writing. To begin with, I had a number of images and ideas I was interested in exploring, but the precise details of how the story would evolve eluded me. I had some notes, but beyond these the future was a blank. I did, however, have a reasonably clear sense of the novel's opening, and this is where I began. The act of transcribing my vision into prose (describing my protagonist, deciding what she should do) generated further ideas, and this gathered in momentum as the writing progressed. The process can also be retroactive. Ideas that emerge in the course of later episodes can flesh out or resolve difficulties in earlier passages. In this sense I might have started the novel anywhere — a point that may prove helpful to new writers uncertain where to begin. My advice would be: start with what you have, then work backwards and forwards from this. You might even discover a new angle in the process. Many writers reorder their work with a view to greater clarity or increased reader interest.

A further formal element that evolved in the course of writing was the arrangement of the text on the page. Reading, unless you are a braille reader or listening to someone reading aloud, is a visual activity and, in addition to seeking graphic parallels for my thematic exploration of fantasy and reality, I found myself experimenting with layout and even typeface in other ways. At one point in the novel Melanie watches television, flicking channels between a TV game show and episodes from the film _Superman_. I decided to place what she sees inside square frames recalling its screen origin. I enjoyed the resultant visual echo of my aquarium motif.

> Superman wrestled a giant octopus. Chained to a bed in a downtown garage a blond woman screamed.

CLICK.

> Which perfume does your wife wear?

CLICK.

> The blond woman's eyes dilated in terror as her captor tied a handkerchief across her mouth.

CLICK.

> How does your husband most like to make love?

CLICK.

> Superman plunged his knife into the eye of the octopus. Blood stained the television screen red.

One of the main problems I encountered in the course of writing involved those episodes I decided were structurally and thematically necessary to my narrative. With hindsight, I realize that the majority of these can be divided into two groups. One group centres on the happiness Melanie feels towards the end of her stay in Paris. Was this difficulty to convey happiness a personal one? I thought of the books I like best. Almost all are tragedies of one sort or another. Toni Morrison's *Beloved*. Gabriel Josipovici's *Contre-Jour*. R.M. Lamming's *The Notebook of Gismondo Cavalletti*. Even the 'happy' endings that came to mind — Julian Barnes'

Metroland, Anita Brookner's _Hotel du Lac_ — rely for their effect on a subtle irony. Is happiness a general human failing? Or is it more simply that happiness is something to be lived? The second group is gender specific. Melanie's initial disasterous attempts to form a sexual relationship are countered in the novel by a brief but passionate affair on holiday in Northern France. In the notes I made for this section, I planned for a lengthy exploration of Melanie's sexual awakening in prose that would be both sensual and erotic. In practice I found this impossible to write. The difficulty was partly linguistic. Looking back over discarded drafts, I realize that my narrative is either too clinical or expressed in language that still strikes me as scatological. Where are the novels, I ask myself, that convey women's sexual experience? It is not only the absence of words that prevents us but centuries of cultural conditioning. Mary is after all (let us not forget) a virgin.

Rewriting can sometimes provide solutions to problems, though here again the rules vary. One writer I know works on a roll of paper refusing to reread or rewrite what she has written. Other writers (James Joyce for instance) spend days wrestling with a sentence until they feel it has found its final form. I have sympathies with Joyce, though have long since relinquished any pretension to a single one of my sentences achieving perfect shape. This does not mean I don't rewrite, I do, but I've learnt that with limited time at my disposal investing a morning in a sentence is not only unproductive (the chances are I'll look at it next day and _still_ see room for improvement) but bogs me down at a certain point in the narrative — and threatens to keep me there. Writing is a craft as well as a desire which improves with practice, and I know too many potentially good writers who never see a project through to its conclusion because they become stuck at a certain point and lose the courage to go on. I believe wholeheartedly in the just-get-it-down approach. You can always rework what you have written and writing is itself the best teacher. The process might even furnish unexpected solutions (you might discover, for example, that the laboriously wrought

passage you squandered all those weeks on is irrelevant and
needs to be cut). The exhilaration of ending can itself rekindle
the energy to prune and rewrite.

In *The Aquarium*, my initial notes were gradually superceded
by those made in the process of composition. The increasing
attention to structure meant that large-scale changes were
kept to a minimum. Only one episode was cut completely,
though several which had suggested themselves in the course
of writing were included. Smaller revisions, such as the
redrafting and rewriting of specific sections, were more frequent. Sometimes the rewriting affected an entire episode.
Other alterations were more local, as in this sentence describing my protagonist gazing out to sea.

> Melanie shaded the sun from her eyes with the flat of her
> hand and watched a group of fishing trawlers, trailing a
> private flotilla of seagulls that bobbled cork-like on the
> water.

The sentence began with a more prosaic account of what
Melanie saw.

> As she stood on the cliff and looked out to sea, she could see
> a dotted group of small islands, a group of fishing trawlers
> throwing their nets behind them into the sea, a group of
> seagulls bobbing on the water like corks as they swam
> behind the trawlers.

The problems are immediately apparent. Not only is there an
awkward repetition of group ('group of small islands', 'group
of fishing trawlers', 'group of seagulls'), but the reiteration of
'trawlers' in such a short sentence is unnecessary. These
difficulties, however, are minor when compared to the
disasterous conjunction between 'sea' and 'see' ('as she looked
out to sea . . . she could see . . . behind them into the sea').
Clearly this had to go. The correlation between the group of
islands and group of fishing trawlers also began to appear not
only awkward but irrelevant. It was important to me to
describe Melanie's new environment and I needed to give
details of what she saw, but the 'dotted group of small
islands' was weak. I decided I needed to write more about the
islands and I tried, embroidering an image of perspective

based on the contrast between land and sea. But as the role of the islands in the sentence increased, the fishing trawlers lost their place and I had become attached to the seagulls bobbing about on the water. I endeavoured to work the gulls into a separate sentence, but it somehow lost its effect. So the islands were sacrificed. I was then left with the problem of how to describe the gulls. 'Trailing seagulls' didn't work, but I didn't want to resort to a repetition of 'group' having already used it for the trawlers. I tried 'flock', but this suggested land, and what I liked about the gulls was their absurd bobbing movement on the water. Perhaps 'fleet' was better? 'Fleet', however, made the image too explicit and competed in size with the trawlers when what I wanted to convey was a sense of the birds' brave ridiculousness. 'Flotilla' was presumably coined via 'flock' and 'fleet', but I liked its sound and its associations. I had now introduced a series of 'l's ('trailing', 'flotilla', 'seagulls', 'like') and it seemed appropriate to continue the movement by adding an 'l' to bobbed, especially as I enjoyed the way 'bobbled' conjured the comic indestructibility of plastic ducks.

A vital element in the way we perceive ourselves and others entails our unconscious fantasies and fears as these are revealed to us in dreams. In _The Aquarium_, I was interested in exploring this other life in its relation to identity and in its potential transformation of fictional form. The first dream occurs while Melanie is still at home.

> That night she dreamed of a circus and herself with a whip alone in the centre of the ring. . . . The whip fired like a pistol shot and out into the ring came her mother and father. . . . Her mother was dressed as a poodle, a pink frill round her waist . . . as for her father, good heavens, her father was an automatic tea-dispenser, steel wheels and levers gleaming as he sent cups of brown liquid flying out in all directions. . . . The music changed to a titillating strip-tease, and . . . Melanie peeled off her school tunic and tie. . . . Encouraged by the applause, she removed more and more layers of clothing, her girl guide's uniform, her church dress, an angel's outfit her mother had made for the school play.

This early dream conveys the ambivalence of Melanie's dilemma since, despite her role as ring-master and possessor of the whip, she remains subject to the wishes of the crowd. In addition to highlighting a key thematic point, the dream also provided an opportunity to move beyond the constraints of realist writing and create a more dynamic account. I enjoyed inventing images that would reveal a different dimension to the people in Melanie's life, and the fantasy and humour added texture to the writing. This first dream is nevertheless expressed in straightforward prose and clearly demarcated as such.

As the novel progressed, I began to experiment with different ways of incorporating dreams. Whether or not we believe in the machinations and influence of the unconscious, we have all experienced, at one time or another, the intense 'reality' of fantasies and fears. The relegation of such forces to designated areas of dream-narrative seemed a falsification. Much has now been written on the controversial subject of women's writing, but if we equate masculinity with the desire for homogeneity and control then any *other* desire to explore ambiguity and dis-order can perhaps accurately be labelled feminine. Whatever its theoretical appellation however, the increasingly blurred distinction between dream and reality produced both a thematic parallel and formal vehicle through which to explore Melanie's quest for identity. In this next extract, Melanie's affair with Philippe is expressed in a sequence which both is and is not a dream. It is left to the reader to decide where truth and reality lie. The episode connects to an earlier 'dream' quoted here on page 99, in which Melanie imagines taking part in a television game that, in the way of dreams, resurfaces a number of incidents, objects and phrases already introduced into the text. The manuscript that appears here refers to a romance Melanie wrote in code as a child, and the radio and mug are objects she has seen advertised. Melanie's story is counterpointed in the novel by that of her employer Madame Robert, and one of the phrases comes from Madame Robert's diary which Melanie stumbles upon by accident. This weave of dream and reality provided a fertile form through which to analyze the ways fantasy shapes perception, and enabled the foregrounding of the more destructive elements of Melanie's desire without recourse to the (masculine?) device of authorial decree.

Don't you see that's just it, Philippe said, stubbing his cigarette out in the ashtray, I don't want you to wait for me. You're always hanging around, good grief you never do anything unless I'm there.

Philippe's eyes were dark holes in which Melanie felt herself drowning.

She had often imagined Philippe cruel.

She had never imagined he would hate her.

She wore a long white robe, her loose hair flowing like a shawl. . . . A young man with dark eyes was leading her through an enchanted garden towards a river. . . . At the water's edge the young man lifted her onto a raft. . . . She let her hands trail in the water, abandoning herself to the river's momentum and the pull of the oarsman's stroke.

All at once, a whisper rose from the water.

You brought me flowers.

I can speak again.

And she knew her fate.

She was Ophelia, beautiful Ophelia, condemned to drown in her madness and her grief.

As she realised this a soft peace descended over the river. The peace of doves and devotion. The blind oblivion of undying love.

Her hair was the green-blue of the ocean.

Her eyes were pearls.

She surrendered, drowning.

Goodnight sweet lady.

Since she had nothing left to fear, Melanie removed her blindfold. The glare of lights startled her and she looked at the oarsman in surprise. But the oarsman, whom she instantly recognized as Philippe, was struggling to steady the raft against an eddy of microphones and electric cables. . . .

Philippe anchored the raft to box number seven and Melanie saw that the sky was a thick pane of glass. She caught hold of a key that was a bright orange fish and handed it to Philippe. . . . He opened the box and took out a coded manuscript. For some reason it seemed familiar to Melanie. He unpacked a transistor radio and a mug commemorating the Queen's anniversary. . . .

A farewell toast.

From the bottom of the box, Philippe removed two rolls of white bandage. He read through the instructions in the manuscript and wound one of the rolls around his neck, signalling to Melanie to copy him. When the white chokers were almost in place he tied the remaining end of his bandage to hers. . . . The lights swivelled onto the raft, transforming it into a miniature stage. Melanie looked at Philippe, but all she could see were the irradiated reflections of her own chokered image in his eyes. She was shackled to him by a white cord of umbilical dependence. . . .

Finally she understood.

He wanted her to dance for him.

Wielding the rein that bound them, Philippe dictated her movements. . . . Melanie whirled and span, spiralling the cord tighter ever tighter as she danced. . . . She fell, stumbled to her feet, tried to leap, but the cord that held her was now so tight she could hardly breathe. She looked at him in dumb, suffocating silence, begging him to help her, release her, give her life.

But Philippe was on his knees, gasping for air, transfixed by her spiralling whiteness, fettered by his vision of power.

She knew they were destroying each other.

And that the dance would go on until one of them was dead.

So the fortune teller was right.

It wasn't the water she had to fear after all.

```
 X |   | O
---|---|---
   | O |
---|---|---
 O |   | X
```

The image of an aquarium as a title and motif for my novel had a strange codicil to it. Inspiration for the narrative was partly autobiographical, and the initial notes I made drew on my childhood and adolescent experiences. Yet to what point are even our own stories created from those we are given? To what extent do our fictions reproduce existing codes? As a woman born in the 50's, a student through the feminist campaigns of the 70's, living now in the 90's, I wonder what our stories for the next century will be? Will they, as in this past decade, be new versions of the old? In other words the same. Or will we finally rewrite them? I wonder. . . .

When my father was six years old, his father, who worked for a brewery, became manager of a pub in the West Midlands. As the eldest child my father was given a room of his own in the pub attic. For some reason the room terrified my father, and at night he would creep in to sleep with his younger siblings. At length the term of my grandfather's contract expired. On the last day, while the family were loading their belongings, my father darted back into the house. There was a glass case with a fish inside it behind the bar, which my father carried to his room. There he destroyed it, releasing the fish and whatever it was that had upset him.

I did not hear this story until some months after _The Aquarium_ was complete. Is it a coincidence, I ask myself, that in the notes I made for the novel my angry and frightened heroine smashes the aquarium in her employers' living room?

I wonder.

Nicole Ward Jouve

The Red Road

The older you get, the lower you go.

The well gets deeper. The swinging bucket bangs against wet, pitch-black walls. In the inverted space, mounting echoes peal: or toll.

It was my friend Isabelle who first told me about Rimbaud. We were fifteen. Marseille, France, in the fifties. We were pupils at a catholic school. Rome's Index reigned supreme. A lot of writers were in it: taboo. Rimbaud was one of them. Much too wild, too amoral to be studied.

Isabelle was a Protestant. Protestants had been hunted down under Louis XIV. That marked her out for a start. At morning prayers, when we stood in the aisles beside our desks, she proudly crossed her arms and kept silent. A defiant smile hovered on her lips. I was torn between admiration at such daring, and praying for two just in case: the trap-door of hell might open under her feet and swallow her, gold-medal-with-the-descending-dove and all. Hell's maw was wide as we well knew, and with such tokens of witchcraft or heresy around your neck, well! devils were ever ready to grab at your ankles.

Marseille post-World War II: Protestants had been prominent in the French Resistance.

In earlier years, Isabelle and I had shared a defiant passion for Chateaubriand. Chateaubriand, with his appeal to 'orages désirés', was, our literature teacher had made clear, bad company. He had written good books about religion, which redeemed him (but not till after he'd been up to a thing or two, *René* for one, where the hero's love for his sister. . .). Lamartine was recommended: he introduced you to all that was suitable for bourgeois females of our province and generation: nostalgia, a taste for the more sedate aspects of the countryside, modesty, coping with defeat, lack and loss tempered by faith, giving up politics as a bad job, moral indignation ripening with age into resigned contemplativeness. Isabelle had re-

turned after a year's absence. 'Do you still read Chateaubriand?'
I asked. The contemptuous smile appeared. 'Chateaubriand is
just silly', she said. 'It's Rimbaud now I love.'

I got hold of a copy.

'Je m'en allais, les poings dans mes poches crevées', 'I
went on my way, fists in my torn pockets.'

My dream of running away to become a circus acrobat
resurfaced. My inn at the end of the road had the sign of the
Great Bear. Things cracked in my head, my heart, metal
bounced and smashed wood as my imaginary Drunken Boat
tumbled down to sea and the waters rushed in, 'scattering
helm and grappling hook'.

In real life, I went on to develop the suitable feminine
qualities Lamartine had been praised for: nostalgia, passivity,
modesty. . . The nuns had done me to a turn.

Rimbaud stayed with me. I knew lots of his poems, his
lines, by heart. I taught him, with an unavowed passion. I
never knew what to say, or said the daft things one says when
one is trying to be 'professional'. The poetry had its effect, as
poetry will, all by itself. Students would write moving essays.
One of them in particular, at what must have been the right
moment, stuck. Ploughing through a pile of marking, I became entranced: 'On suit la route rouge pour arriver à l'auberge
vide.' 'Les palissades sont si hautes qu'on ne voit que les
cimes bruissantes.'

'You follow the red road to come to the empty inn.' 'The
palisades are so high one can only see the soughing tops.'
These words were meant for me: though obviously they
were also meant for the man who wrote the essay. I could
give him a first class mark, and yet I could never communicate with him at the level we both had inhabited when he
wrote and I read. We are better than we are, than we can ever
say, or do: the poets have sung our deepest, our keenest, our
saddest, our cruellest selves. When we come across them,
it's like coming home. Or as in Cathy's dream in *Wuthering
Heights*: being ejected from the ill-fitting, make-believe
heaven of daily life, upwards into the real home, which is
the hell of the Heights.

'On suit la route rouge pour arriver à l'auberge vide.' I had to spend time inside that line. Lots.

Rimbaud was born in Charleville in 1854. His father had abandoned his mother. She had struggled to bring up the children single-handedly, a stern, some suggest bitter, woman. Rimbaud had been a brilliant pupil, of literature especially, writing amazing letters to his favourite teachers. An early rebel, he several times ran away from home, towards Paris, once at the time of the 1870 Franco-Prussian war. His mother had sent the police after him. But then, eventually, he'd made it to Paris, invited by Verlaine. He had been fêted by the Paris poets, had behaved with unremitting ill-grace, or downright loutishness, and finally ran away to London with Verlaine, making Verlaine leave his young wife Mathilde. Some books tell how, when Rimbaud had been staying with the couple, he'd lain on their bed, deliberately rubbing his muddy boots on their white pillow. . . . In England the two vagabonds had tried it all: alcohol, 'l'absinthe aux verts piliers', 'green-pillared absinth', hallucinogenetic drugs, sex, violence, tramping. And then Rimbaud ran away to the continent pursued by Verlaine, who caught up with him and shot him in the hand in Brussels' main station. Jail for Verlaine. A brief return home for Rimbaud, who wrote *A Season in Hell* in his mother's farmyard barn, howling: or so the story goes. And then, at barely 21, he gave up poetry forever. The rest of his life was spent wandering, with attempts to make money at various louche trades, arms-dealing among others. Some claimed he dabbled in the slave-trade, though that's been disproved. Stories pick him up in Somalia, in the Harar desert with a wounded leg, where gangrene eventually set in. They say that by sheer will-power he got his porters to carry him back to Aden. Then Marseille. Then home. Back to Marseille, near the sea, where his sister — another Isabelle — nursed him. Death. The rough outlines of a life about which I knew as much or as little as the next person. In recent years, the poet Alain Borer, a one time associate of Ginzberg, in a voyage eloquently recounted, sailed with a French TV crew and retraced Rimbaud's East African travels. He found his name carved on one of the pyramids. That's all. The rest was just desert. Photographs of today's desert women. A very few, sparse, business letters. All that's left of the last fifteen years of he who wrote *The Illuminations*. Mr Rimbaud, tradesman. 'Un sieur Rimbaud, négociant.'

And so Rimbaud remains the eternal adolescent. Verlaine called him 'le vagabond aux semelles de vent', 'the vagabond with wind in his soles'.

There were to be neither mountains nor vales in my story. I knew that where Rimbaud had wandered in his youthful escapes from home the landscapes were all flat, the flatlands of the Meuse, the North of France. And yet I knew there was going to be travel through both hell and heaven. Hadn't Rimbaud, for a start, told how he'd spent a season in hell? And more than one. . . Hadn't he been a dying man who survived, went on dying until he caught his death in the Harar desert? And what a hell that survival must have been. . .

He had never known paradise, an essay by Anne Berger that I read at the time in the review *Fruits* reflected. He had never known the 'murmur' of his mother's milk, the 'murmure des voix anciennes'. Ancient voices murmuring. He had never (I reflected, being steeped in Colette at that particular moment), he had never known that paradise which Colette said she had lost, but forever inhabited, 'J'habite à jamais un paradis que j'ai perdu'. What Rimbaud had never had, he had never been able to lose. He had never been able to go through mourning 'faire son deuil'. Life had ever been impossible for him: he had never been able to come to terms with loss. Anne Berger never mentioned Colette. But those were the terms in which I heard what she had written. And so the idea arose: what would have happened if Rimbaud had met Colette? What if she, whose work re-invented mothering through the figure of her own mother Sido, had been a fey child, both adolescent child and her own re-imagined mother? Could I imagine a young female who would combine the two figures Colette wrote and re-wrote, the confident, zany nurturer Sido who knows the ways of plants and beasts, and the girl-child

who freely roams the woods at dawn? Could I imagine a little
female who could do some holding because she herself feels
so confidently, so lovingly held? In *My Mother's House*, the
little girl wants to be a mariner when she grows up. She stays
in the garden one evening as the darkness descends, confront-
ing the terrors of the barbed yuccas: then catches sight of her
mother's thimble by the lamp indoors, and rushes to safety,
pulled in by the thread. . . . Could I invent a little girl who'd
do better mothering than her own mother: who'd let the
wandering 'child' go, but in such a way that one day he might
find his way back? Could she be the explorer who stays still
but enables the one she holds by an invisible Ariadne thread
to both voyage and be sure to come home? Thus the vagabond
in her might have found release from her shackles. . . . Thus
they might both have been released. Self-sufficient in the end
like Tournier's twins in *The Meteors*: 'Thy firmness makes
my circle just/And makes me end where I began'.

What if Rimbaud in his wanderings had met with such a
female? Would he have chosen 'life', been saved from the
endless compulsion to voyage, and return, and never stay
still, and never find? Might he (who in his adolescence had
written 'Vowels', A, E, I, U, O; a poem that travelled through
the alphabet with its train of barely visible, barely audible
consonants, for A was for Alpha and O for Omega, and the
other letters never mentioned for they were not pure voices,
they were just attendant articulation), might he have been
relieved from the compulsion to go from the beginning to the
end, and again, amid the ever thinning ghosts of consonants?
Might he then never have begun the final treck, the trip from
A to Z, Aden to Zanzibar, one end of the world to the other?
The trip which never went further than A, than Aden — which
kept him returning home again and again, to Europe, the
'flache/Noire et froide', the cold black puddle on which an
eternal child keeps launching a paper boat as frail as a May
butterfly, 'un bateau frêle comme un papillon de Mai'? Kept
returning to the narrow, black sunless mother, Charleville the
home town, and back again to the sea, the un-nursing Medi-
terranean? What an irony that the man died near the beginning

of birth, close to the sea, in a hospital called '*La Conception*'. . . .

If Rimbaud had met up with a child-Colette, would he have been able to make 'a circle just' rather than burn up in four years all possibilities of writing, and of life? Would there have been a sunny, not a 'sunless sea' for one in a long line of Khans, and he the speediest and most scorched of them all? (And would there have been no more poetry either?). Dawn would not have fallen at the same time as the child at the edge of the wood. There would have been a noon, and an evening, and a crossing of the wood. The inn would not have been empty, as for Rimbaud it ever remained.

Of course Rimbaud could never have met Colette. She was a baby when he wandered north of that native Burgundy of hers, she was barely more than a toddler when he gave up poetry forever. The rural but well-read adolescent who had spent such a happy childhood in Saint-Sauveur-en-Puisaye, and who now had a crush on Parisian *belle-lettriste* Willy (whom she was soon to marry) may never have read the discreet notice that announced the death in the hospital of La Conception, Marseille, of a 'sieur Rimbaud, négociant'. The hospital where my father worked, just down the street where I spent my childhood and grew up. . . .

It had to be his voice. There never was any doubt about that. He might have written 'Je est un autre' 'I am another', and in my own way I knew what he meant. But what a powerful 'I', even when he used the third person, even when he said 'on', you, one. 'On suit la route rouge pour arriver à l'auberge vide'. How could one deviate from that?

There had to be deviation though. I was female. I wasn't him. I was pushing fifty. He had been an adolescent boy.

I've read that tight-rope walkers can balance when they let go, when some inner sense takes over from the conscious mind. The voice I wanted could not be sounded by trying, by imitation, intention. I had to listen to the echoes of Rimbaud's voice in me. I had to be a wild adolescent male, I had to release the unappeased youth in me: and why not? Who says he wasn't there somewhere inside me, the 'enfant accroupi plein de tristesse', 'the crouching child full of sadness' who never left Rimbaud from the days of his Northern boyhood to his writing _Le Bateau ivre_ — to that last trip to Aden, where he would dig a pit with a stick by the pathside when his Abyssinian carriers put down his litter, so he could shit as his own man?

I had a pleasurable shock when I heard Christiane Veschambre, a French novelist, at a Paris conference on Sexual Difference, talk of the 'virilité de l'écriture' in my story, then called '_Un Détour d'Arthur_', which I had earlier shown to her. She talked of the 'vigour' of the narrator's language, of its 'energetic and elastic rhythm', of its 'nomadic young boy's gait'. (She's since then published the essay in the _Cahiers Jungiens de Psychanalyse_, No 75, pp. 12–17). She reflects most interestingly on the way Bachelard has used Jung's concepts of the 'animus', i.e. woman's unconscious masculine part, and the 'anima', or man's unconscious feminine part. Pierre Solié calls them 'the psychosexual complement' in both man and woman. I was struck by this, having worked for the past ten to fifteen years, first in France then in England, in an intellectual world steeped in the fashionableness of Freud and Lacan. They were so influential upon feminist theory, were it but as the windmills to tilt at. Part of me evidently knew that masculinity and femininity exist in us as something other than two enemy frontier towns, one displaying the notice 'penis envy' over its congregational church, the other with 'womb envy' as its saloon sign, and 'fear of the castrating mother' writ large over its funeral parlour. Between them ran a river called 'mirror stage', which little boys crossed triumphantly as part of Male City's initiation rite, while the little denizens of Female City floundered in it dreadfully, becoming so captivated by their watery reflection that they lost their little totems amid the eddies. It was startling to find that there had been all along 'theories' such as Jung's, that didn't bear out such polarization. I had indeed read Bachelard's _Poétique de la rêverie_, many years before. 'Who writes?' he asks, 'animus or anima?' He does not answer his own question, speaking instead of books written or read 'in animus' or 'in anima', whatever the 'sex' of their author/reader. But he does stress how writing which engages some of our deepest, that is, most unknown forces, engages the Other in us: our Other. Animus and anima are, Christiane Veschambre insists, *unconscious* figures. They pertain to our secret, inner psyche. 'Their origin is archaic, and because of all this, they cannot be confounded with what is sometimes referred to as bisexuality', a term that has superficial, almost 'behaviourist' implications. For a woman to gain access to her animus, to the 'stranger in herself', a 'salutary cruelty' may be necessary. Giving up on certain forms of selfhood. Reaching towards a 'singular anonymity'.

There had been some conscious experimentation in what I had written, especially in the encounter between Arthur (he is never called Rimbaud: of course he is not Rimbaud) and Tabby, little Colette who, of course, is never anything like little Sidonie-Gabrielle (her name came from a weird parodic Rimbaud piece, 'Un Coeur sous une soutane', in which a seminarist worships a girl called Tabbithina). Mindful of one Hélène Cixous essay 'Castration or Decapitation?', in which she claims that throughout Western culture woman is always found in bed, often as Sleeping Beauty, I had reversed the roles and made my Tabby discover my Arthur asleep, and watch him wake. But then, she is the one who puts him up, in her house, lets him travel from cellar to attic. . . . She has the power, yet they're each in each other's power. . . . Surprising how swiftly good intentions went overboard. Surprising also how much a male remains a male however much you play with gender roles. I'm sure that this resistant and — yes — elastic maleness had to do with something in me — call it animus — having taken over. I keep trying to put it into words, other words, to say, 'he is so game, so complete — there is simplicity in his desire, his acceptance of what comes to him, his readiness'. But then words slip, don't they?, like this whole impossible gender vocabulary.

I wrote very slowly, with talismans: with a green parchment pencil, on a green-and-black parchment-covered notebook my daughter had brought me back from Florence. In a garden in the Cévennes in which everything was green-black: lawns and fountains under the huge plane-trees. Green would be the counterpoint to red. It would spell out, it would realize the absence of colour from the 'cimes bruissantes', 'the soughing tops' over the high palisades which you only ever see through their sound. Quite uncharacteristically for me, I erased and re-wrote, erased and re-wrote again, instead of producing my usual scribbled and overlaid and barely legible pages. It was a tribute to the beauty of the notebook, the shelter it was giving us. Even when Arthur failed to scale the walls of the strange domain, I did not get downcast. We were safe. . . . Except, of course, for the red road, the beast that like the beasts at the beginning of *The Divine Comedy* bar the poet's way.

Did that stop us from being safe?

The Red Road

One

> You follow the red road to come to the empty inn.
> Arthur Rimbaud
> 'Enfance'

I walked under the sky, it was pale. And who knows at what point I took the red road. I had to go left. I had no choice: the road on my right ran through fields of sugar beet, towards a horizon of sugar beet. I hate substitutes. I hate Empires: they have scrambled the routes to real sugar, oh my lost Indies. The beet leaves spread scabies on the flat fields. I'll unearth them I said. I'll turn into a million moles, I'll grub them all up. The mother of sugar rattled in my ears. Forests of canes, filtering the suns. Fibres spurted their juice into my mouth. I chewed them like tits. Splinters got stuck under my nails as I tried to unfurl the stems:

I wanted papyrus out of them. I would write in spit on sugar scrolls. A new Baby Moses, I drifted in my cane cradle from the Nile to the West Indies. I floated past the giant dugs of mother whales as gleefully as under the luminous arcs of the dolphins. The suns had roasted me to such a turn that I was black when I landed in Martinique, gorged with papyrus leaves and the milky gruel of the sperm whales.

In disgust at the beet, I had gone left. I walked, my fists in my pockets and the Atlantic in my nostrils. My mouth was full of the tropics. It was moons now since I had passed under the winy shadow of the pillars of Hercules. My jacket was tight. My wrists jutted from the sleeves, bony and red like my hands. The servant at the drinking den, the servant with tits warm as the ham she'd brought me, had stared at them all through the meal. I pulled at my sleeves. And then I ceased to pull, because the wine was tart and the radishes red and white like her mouth on her face and she was big-hearted and soft-bellied; and on the road to the inn there had been bags of fertilisers blue as the methylene my mother used to paint on my mouth ulcers. And fields of yellow mustard-seed in which you could have drowned city squares.

I walked. The wind blew gnats on my glottis. I swallowed them. I felt them go down, puny shipwrecks. I imagined their voyage, from the spittly banks of my Nile to my marshy brown Indies. I even dreamt of stools punctuated with black.

I skidded. I looked at the road where for a long time now I had been walking. It was red. Tulip-red, satiny, trellissed with brilliant veins. Every step a risk. To slip, to crush. I wanted the harpoon feet of wasps to hook into the tender flesh of the petal road. But my boot studs were a memory of long ago. The boots gaped at the toes. Gravel pierced the soles. Only the strings held them. I pulled them tight at night, I strummed them. They sang better than cats' guts.

Then I saw the grass.

Green, as far as the horizon. Nothing but grass. As far as the horizon. Lush. Green, as Judas is a traitor, and the thunder sun, orange. Insolently green, as far as the eye could see.

Beyond where the eye could see. It ate up sight. Greedy-green, gorged on life yet famished. The green of a land whose belly was even greedier than mine. It was waiting for me. Suddenly I knew. And the road, red. As red as the fields were green. The red and green could have been a delicious pain.

If I could have looked at them. From somewhere else. If I could not have been there. But I had to walk. Every step on the red, I feared to skid. I knew. The Northern Plain. It had drunk the blood of millions of men. It would drink the blood of millions more. All the invasions had passed over it. Been halted there sometimes. Attila. Where my horse treads, he'd say, grass never grows again. Yet it had grown. Grown all too well. It was green, insolently. It was a land which had drunk, had become bloated, like the obese adolescents I beat to a pulp at school. Me the thin the weedy one. With my bony peasant's wrists. The road was a sewer, a wide clotted sewer which had drained the Northern fields for thousands of years. I had seen the soldier in his green hole. I now knew where his blood had finished up. How much liquid can flow from a man's body.

I sweated. I was in an enchanted world, where none but me perhaps had ever ventured. And they knew I was there. The plain was bare as a belly. Not a tree, not a post, not even a bush. I almost longed for the beets. Grass swelled on my right. Curved on my left. And yet in the distance the dark stain of a wood.

I remembered a tale. The boy must flee with the princess, he carries her on his back across a meadow. At the slightest graze, the foot scratched by a stone or a thistle, as soon as blood beads on the skin, the grass begins to moan. From blade to blade the mutter spreads. The grass groans, it growls, it screams, it howls. It calls for the ogre. The meadow itself is an ogress. The ogre sallies from his tower, he brandishes a club. The meadow screams, she opens her mouths, soon it is all mouths that gape in waves, larger and larger they turn into furrows, ditches, six feet by two; I knew — as a child I had the book — that they were pits where you might bury a man. The mouths open, they close, chew, swallow, the earthy guts beneath rumble and travail, the mouths are legion, they're men-eaters, the meadow is a cemetery, her mouths open wave after wave then close gape again, there beneath your feet, the boy leaps, jumps. Can't remember the end. Perhaps the ogre falls into one of the mouths and fights with the meadow his ogress, a giant toad swallowed by a grass-snake. Or else the princess has a balm which heals the boy's wounds and the blood ceases to flow and the grass to drink and it stops screaming and the waves smooth down and the boy and princess escape. I looked at my boots. Scabs on the old wounds, and new blisters, the flesh raw-red, and I knew that this grass would be my grave if I dared venture into it. Left, right, ahead and at my back, the man-eating grass sea. Through it there meandered the red road, my fate.

I turned around. I who always went ahead, I who bit into everything, the wind, the breasts, the beasts, I turned back.

And saw it. The beast. Over there, where I had first stepped onto the red road, far away in the distance but clear as the day so dead flat the plain, a wolf was lying across the road. I saw it rise the moment I turned. Front legs, hind legs. Ears pointing towards me. Lean as myself. He was looking at me. I took a step towards him. One. A shiver ran over his spine. A wind shudder over a meadow. One more step. His fangs were bared. Spittle made them shine, white pebbles wet with the sea. Another step, and I perceived a growl. Muffled, a latent thunder in a summer sky. The plain was so bare that the thunder would instantly find me. I halted. The growling stopped. I took another step, it started again. I saw the beast as if it had been close, was upon me. I knew his hunger. His leaping, and how it would knock me to the ground, the hot breath and the saliva running on my face, the rumbling throat and the jumble of our wrestling. My fists were full of the flabby neck folds, the thick white hair as I laboured to throttle him. Ivory and horn tore at me, mixed with the caresses of warm fur. My knees and boots hammered at ribs, the gap between the ribs, each vulnerable as the fontanel on a baby's skull. Oh for a penknife to burst it, to stab through to the heart that beat faster than mine! I knew the jaws snapping over my throat, the sun fringed with orange, the sweet flooding of blood that would deafen, then clot, thickening the road's crust. I paused.

We were staring at each other. He was panting faster than me. His breath, his heart, his legs, faster than mine. But he was quiet. On his haunches, eyes rivetted to mine, he had all the time in the world.

I challenged him. A stallion cornered by the pack, I stamped on the ground, and neighed. Enough to hole the sky. In the furnace of my guts, all the bellows got going. Every cell of my lungs inflated to bursting, emptied themselves, spewed their wind towards my brass pipe. It vibrated. A cry, hiiiiii, which whistled like the chests of consumptives, the veins that pop, the pockets into which the blood seeps. The whistlings of my childhood nights. In bed listening to the others, in the end your ears are full to bursting as if the north wind had filled them. I vomited, I spat out my cry, far out from me, so it would stain the sky.

The wolf still watched me. He did not blink, did not shiver. You might have thought that he was deaf. He had been given the order to block my way back. He blocked my way back.

I turned around again. Looking backwards as far as my neck would turn. The jaw clamped shut, the hair slowly smoothed down. With the corner of my eye I saw the haunches lowering to the ground.

I took two steps. Stopped again. Looked over my shoulder. The beast had sat down, but he trembled, nostrils flared, ears straining. He was keening to be upon me. One step, two steps towards him, and he would be erect, tail whipping his lean sides, hams straining to trot, to spring. I took up the road again.

Each step my violation. Not just my feet, each time they met the road, squirming as they feared to slip, to sink into what might, any second, have turned liquid. Every hair in my body stood up in dread of falling on, into, the red wet.

I summoned memories to my aid. The inn where the dark-haired hostess had fed me black pudding, had drawn stout for me. Black pudding, black guinness, its froth the colour of coffee-and-milk. I stared at the mug. You could see the sea through the window. Opaque. It sizzled, like the lead of my toy

soldiers when I melted them in the ladle at the flame of my
mother's stove. The mother screamed, 'You vile boy! my soup
ladle! your father's lead soldiers!'. But the sea was cold, and it
was foam now that burst into bubbles, and the sea was wide, or
so I thought, it was the North sea at Scarborough. The borough
of the scar. I took myself for a soldier just returned from the war.
The inn was close to the ruins of the castle, on the soft-turfed
cliff. The guinness was as sweet as milk. It was the earth's black
milk, milk drawn with the plough, whipped with a thresher,
fermented in vats: men's milk. Near my table, the hostess's arse
shook, its drapery of ample skirts closed tight like church
curtains. She was polishing the floor with a red wax called
Cardinal. 'This floor's a beauty,' the hostess was saying, 'it lasts
and lasts. Do you know what it's made of?' I was staring at the
sea through the window. The panes were framed in lead. I
wanted to scrape it off with my knife. Melt it all down, the old
world, everything. Let it all go to the sea of melted lead at the
bottom of the cliff, in its ladle of old earth. 'Believe me if you
will,' the hostess was saying, 'it's made of bull's blood mixed
with horse hair. You let it dry, it lasts longer than wood, it's
warmer than stone and you polish it like tiles.' It was a world
of clotted blood, the floor, the black pudding, the guinness. This
is it, that's what you're walking into now, I told myself. Have
a little stomach.
     (. . .)

     He continues walking on the red road. There is a path to
     the right, leading to a walled garden. He follows it: he makes
     a detour. The walls are so high you can only see the soughing
     tops of the trees. All day long he tries to scale the walls, find
     an entrance. He goes round: no way in. At night, exhausted,
     he falls asleep on a heap of stones at the foot of the wall.

The sun was there. On my face. It must have gone around. It
was on the other side, dawn-white, and made me sneeze.
     I opened my eyes. White things everywhere. On a branch,
perched above me. Their eyes plumb into my eyes. A white
cat, flat along a sycamore branch. A little girl in a white apron
on the same branch, propped against the trunk. They had

watched me sleep, they were watching me wake. The eyes of the little girl were sea-green like those of her cat. The two faces, triangular, cocked to the same side.

I sat up. I shook myself, touched my shoulders, my legs my face, tousled my hair, felt for sore spots, was that me, was I there. It was slower than dreams, and it changed less. I was kneeling now half-way up a mound of stones. The stones from the wall. Stones that had tumbled from the top of the wall. I must have fallen asleep at the very moment I had found the passage, literally gone to sleep on the breach. The landslide was so complete that it formed a gangway over the granite foundation: you could clamber over it. No sentries but this derisory little girl, and her cat. The watch-towers, I knew, deserted. All that barred my way-in were four sea-green eyes, so watchful that I felt ashamed, ashamed that they had watched me sleep.

— Did you come to abduct me, the little girl said.

— Me? Abduct an imp of a girl? You must be out of your wits, I said.

— I am more in my wits than you are, she replied, kicking her cat who stepped forward on the branch, arching her back, in a sudden halo of rainbow light. The little girl stretched more comfortably on her branch, leaning on her elbow. I'm not the one who sleeps on a big heap of uncomfortable stones when there is soft wood grass nearby.

I stood up. It was true: I ached all over.

— At any rate you didn't come to wake me up, the little girl said. I'm the one who has been watching you sleep. And it is the dawn, the cat and I who have awoken you. But of the three dawn came first, and she's the only one that's kissed you.

I was choking with rage.

— I'd like to know who cares about being kissed by a stuck-up baby and her cat.

— You are wrong, she lifted her roguish chin disdainfully. Tina is very good at licking.

She sat astride her branch, which pulled her skirts up. She was bare-foot in her sandals, with calves round as a loaf of good bread.

— Well, she said, and what are you waiting for?

I scratched my head. Dug my fists into my pockets. The right-hand one was burst alright. Against my left thigh a chunk of bread. It wasn't a dream, but I was being detoured. Already it was no longer my story: but if I stepped over that wall it would be someone else's.

(He steps over the wall. Follows the little girl into the woods. She dives into the undergrowth, surfaces.)

Her small sticky palm was holding up wild strawberries.

— Taste, she said.

I tasted. Barely warmed by her fist, they burst against my teeth, flooding my palate with their tart scent. Pink as her gums and tongue that laughed in pleasure at my pleasure. Ah the taste of those first strawberries I still have it at the root of my nostrils, the corrals from which saliva springs. I found that I was hungry, so famished I could eat the wood, all its birds, the sun itself. It was my turn to dive in among the wild leaves and lift the green-toothed dais, in the shade of which shelters the most compact taste-scent in the world: the green-white, pink, rosy red berries, dotted like doll's thimbles, bending under their impish green caps at the end of slender strong stems. I raised their chins, the riper ones yielded like the beloved to the lover, clop, a tiny 'clop', the sound of an imp's tongue, and my teeth were irrigated with pink, rose-red juices, from the loveliest mouth in the world. I was hungry so hungry I went flat on my belly. I crawled I gobbled the strawberries amid the green, I rubbed my snout on the earth, (. . .) I was hungry so hungry. For sure, never have the gods eaten nectar equal to the taste of those wild strawberries among which I crawled nose and mouth forward.

The little girl — Tabby — takes him then to a spring to drink. She tumbles him into the water-hole. He swims about, emerges clean. She then takes him on a long walk through the woods to her house, asleep in the noon-day sun. She smuggles him in through the cellars, leads him up to the attic, where she keeps him — a day? a year? He sleeps with strange toys. There is a dove-cote in the next attic. Sometimes when he wakes up Tabby is cuddled up against him. She brings him food. One day she takes him downstairs, to the dining-room. He fears devoration. He thinks he's fallen in with ogresses. He makes violent love to Tabby, to gain control, get his own back, who knows? A plump little lady, the mother, comes in. She is indignant. He turns against her, against Tabby. Then mother and daughter join up to chase him away from the house and enclosed garden. He runs in panic through the heaving green grass all the way back to the red road.

Two

Anyone who has ever completed a novel or a volume of poetry or a play or an autobiography, anything involving that interplay of conscious and unconscious, self and 'singular anonymity' which Christiane Veschambre talks about, will know this: the sources of the text are so diverse (many of them not known; and sometimes understood only years after the writing, sometimes never) that attempting to say 'this is where this comes from' is futile. I can now see things in my *Arthur* I didn't see at the time of writing. Further things became visible, or changed intriguingly in translation. For the book was written in French. Thus the wolf, though 'le loup', masculine, was often called 'la bête', feminine: 'elle' did this and that. In English it became a he. Something was altered. The imagined French fight between boy and beast was between two creatures of disproportionate strength, the one — Arthur — coolly calculating his chances and deciding that without a weapon he was sure to lose, the other (strangely confirmed in its furriness and otherness and gender ambiguity by being both an '*il*' and an '*elle*') simply determined to make Arthur keep walking the red road, or be killed. That was his mission, as in a journey into the underworld or in Tolkien-type fantasy land. No one knew why he was there or who'd sent him. I certainly didn't. That was what happened, that was the way it was. Becoming a he, the wolf acquired stronger or different sexual connotations. 'Il se dressa' became 'he stood erect'. . . . As a result Arthur became bizarrely . . . feminized? Vulnerable, possibly afraid of sex, certainly of that kind of male sexuality — the encounter with a stronger male. I do not know what to make of this, except that now, thinking of Rimbaud's homosexuality, his affair with Verlaine, I begin to understand how the only role Rimbaud ever found acceptable was the male one. I also re-read 'Le Coeur volé' in a different way: there are hints that destructive things happened to the adolescent as he was going round barns or among the Paris defenders at the time of the Commune . . . 'Mon coeur triste bave à la poupe/Mon coeur volé de caporal. . .'. He loathed what's called feminization. Within the damned couple, in *A Season in Hell*, he is 'the infernal husband' to Verlaine's 'foolish virgin'. Yet he was much the younger man.

When I say Rimbaud, I mean the real one. Arthur is my lad.

One source I do remember. The house and garden have connotations of the earthly paradise, not just on account of Colette having used the word for her childhood home and country: because paradise does mean enclosed garden in Persian, and my childhood reading and imagination were full of such 'secret gardens', fascination with Provençal walled gardens. But more specifically Arthur's expulsion from paradise I owe to a late story by Colette, *Le Tendron* (*The Tender Shoot*). In it she settles accounts with the mature male seducers of her youthful *Claudine* books, and she puts pay to her own attraction, as a young girl, to first husband Willy. In *My Apprenticeships* she describes that attraction, which she claims many very young girls feel, as a restless curiosity about sex, a craving for corruption. The satisfaction of this craving, she adds, is its own punishment.

Le Tendron is told by an ageing Don Juan to the overall narrator, one now house-bound Madame Colette. He only fancies very young girls. Once while staying with friends he finds his way through the woods to a derelict estate, with crumbly walls easily breached. There he meets Rosette, an adolescent with a ravishing rosy complexion. She is fascinated by him, heady with her own youth, keen to know sex. One night when he's actually entered the house, intent on what you might call business (till now they've met in the grounds, and dallied, and kissed), a plump lady, in looks very

Sido-like, interrupts. She scolds him, calls him a thief. To the would-be seducer's surprise, the young girl sides with her mother. They chase him away, hunt him through the woods out of the domain, pelting him with stones. He feels he has escaped with his life.

In her late fictions Colette sometimes invented fairy-tale happy endings for the script of her youth. She had married middle-aged *roué* Willy, who prostituted her (and very willing was she, bemused but also keen to play the part) through and as Claudine: in the earlier work Claudine is fascinated by and marries the greying Renaud. But in late *Gigi* the adolescent who has been bred to become a courtesan finds a middle-aged but kindly and uncorrupt suitor, who marries her. In *Le Tendron*, the seducer is hunted away by an alliance of mother and daughter. In the earlier *Claudine* novels, the mother was dead.

What captivated me in *Le Tendron* was the revisioning of myths and fables in gender terms. The male protagonist is not chased out of paradise by a male God aided by male Archangel Michael, but by a plump lady and her adolescent daughter. Rosette is also a novel kind of Eve, and she remains in paradise. The fruit of knowledge is knowledge of, and desire for, sex. Neither good nor bad: the author of *The Pure and the Impure* rewrites these terms. What may be impure is greed, the keenness to taste and possess, regardless of what it does to someone or something else — the concealment, the deceit it involves — the destructiveness that could come in the wake of it all. Paradise is female, run and inhabited by females, reconnected to a nurturing, female body. As of course it always was, and is . . . (even when it is a man who bottle-feeds!). If there *is* paradise, that is, rather than purgatory, or as in Rimbaud's case, something like hell. . . .

Arthur is caught apparently seducing the daughter. Mother and daughter do gang up to chase him from paradise. I wasn't only revisioning the Rimbaud script, but also the Colette: it isn't, for Arthur, a case of seduction, but a fear of being eaten, the impulse to lash out and confusedly attack, verbally, sexually, in self-defense. Tabby's appeal to him is not that of the nymphette to the ageing amateur of young flesh, but that of both sister and mother to a lost and hungry child. Perhaps the idea for that goes as far back as my student days in Marseille, when I knew little Algerian girls of seven with their baby brothers strapped on their backs, confidently and relaxedly patting, comforting, and getting on with whatever else, shopping for mom, playing, learning to knit. Arthur also desires Tabby as young, attractive flesh, as companionable playmate — Rimbaud's relation with his sister Isabelle seems to have been the one that, as he lay dying, surfaced as the enduring one. 'Mon enfant ma soeur. . . .'

I could not have formulated it at the time, but now I understand a bit better: it was crucial that the chasing out of Arthur should not be punishment for a sin, a misdeed, but should have something of the impersonality and ordinary cruelty that separation from the mother often has in life. Mother hens chase away their chicks by savagely pecking at them. The chicks don't know what's hit them, they keep coming back. In the end they first dispiritedly, then gamely, start their grown-up destinies as cocks or hens. It was important that Arthur's sexual access to Tabby as mother, his attacking her as 'the bad breast', should be barred: it saves him from the closure of incest, the temptation of sadism. It meant that in the end he could (according, of course, to how the rest of his life went, what choices he made) — meet up with a different Tabby, a little young girl who was just somebody else, but who could re-awaken and answer to, that first love for Tabby-as-mother. It also meant that he had lost, and could mourn. Sure, he could also feel guilty: he had trespassed. Don't we all? But there was something bigger, more indifferent, impersonal, to the losing. It wasn't something that he had done, something to feel guilty for, or ashamed of. It was a matter of separation. It could have been a matter for tragedy — had we been in another story.

All this I can see now. When I wrote I was groping my way.

There was another major revisioning in process. As I was mulling over this novella, it became the counterpart, the obverse side, to another, which I was also writing. I thought of them in terms of Mallarmé's opposition between life and death, day and night. He conceived at the same time his sunny, life-loving faun who loses the nymphs and sings, in 'L'Après-Midi d'un faune', and his ice-bound, narcissistic, sterile 'Herodiade'. Arthur was my faun. My Herodiade was a Salome of sorts. She ended up on her own. But what did link, and still links, the two novellas, is hunger. My Salome has a huge appetite, and so does my Arthur. He wants to eat everything he meets, including Tabby. he also fears devoration at her hands — her mouth rather — her sex. *Vagina dentata*, castrating mother and all that. He thinks he has been captured by ogresses, like Tom Thumb. Eat or be eaten: that, you could literally say, is his gut feeling. It is also something he has to outgrow before he can meet up with Tabby again. Don't ask me why. I have the learned words to speak it — *vagina dentata* etc. — but it remains for me deep and dark. Narratives such as these are my only means of access. The critical voice remains peripheral.

I have said I was revisioning: Rimbaud and Colette. On reflection that's not the right word. More like 'taking off' from somebody else's bits of language — or rhythm, or one of their story lines — and turning it to my own purposes. These, as I seem to have stressed several times, did entail altering, reversing, experimenting with gender roles. Not satirising them, nor exposing them as decoy, illusion nor rhetoric, as Angela Carter does in much of her seventies fiction. There remain for me in the fiction I write pressing problems of identity. Gender and sex are both in the warp. I am not able to carnivalize as she did. Different compulsions drive me. But hence perhaps the amphibious quality of my *Arthur*. Neither flesh nor fowl. Both realistic tale and fantasy. Mixing high and low, poetry/dream visions and fairy-tale. Longer than story and shorter than novel. I like the term novella.

That length was appropriate. Much too much for a short story, since a life crisis and resolution were at stake. But a full-size novel would have had to turn into a grail-like quest, which would have been hugely out of keeping for a character born of Rimbaud's spume: a poet so gifted with brevity, understatement, punchiness — whose productive life-span had been four years. Texts, in whatever formal capacity — length, music, gait — will insist on being at one with so-called content.

Three

When we conceived the present project, we meant, not only to offer an in-depth account of the process of writing by each of us, detailing the evolution of a piece of writing and critically and theoretically analyzing it, but to produce something of a 'handbook or guide'. I feel I have honoured the first part of this brief: but what kind of a handbook, let alone a guide, is this! If anyone was to read my contributions with the hope that by the end they'd be in a position to write a novella of their own, wouldn't they rightly feel cheated?

Writing stems from desire. No one can tell another person why, what and how to write. Style is the irreducible self, Roland Barthes insisted. Try as you or I might, our prose, or poetry, will be haunted, possessed, by rhythms, paces, compulsive clauses: for instance Proust's countless 'tout de même', 'all the same' . . ., a pause, a hesitancy, a will to consider and weigh all the options, something temperamental, in the blood; it is this that has caused that particular sentence-hanger to make itself felt. There are no recipes, except to go for it, fly in the teeth of fear — boldness and hard graft.

Yet as we each struggle with our particular problems, our particular neuroses and compulsions, useful tips, encouragement and even sometimes illumination can be found through individual tales of effort. I always got solace from Valéry saying in his *Mémoire du poète* that one or two lines may be given, but all the rest have to be worked for — from Balzac in *La Cousine Bette* explaining, with such feeling, that while 'conception' is all dreamy pleasure, 'execution' is a grim task-mistress. As one who dreams up a lot of books, and gets few written, and finds countless pretexts to get away from writing implements, from the doggedly paralyzing white page, the blank screen — I keep reminding myself of Balzac's black-coffee-sodden nights, night after night after night. I think of Colette — of her 'hard gardener's hand, writing'. There is company in that solitude. The single-minded company of those who always look in the same direction. You'll never catch their eye — but you can feel the tension in their backs.

No general guidelines then? Isn't there a lack of modesty, of proper attention to the craft, a wispiness in saying that? Wasn't I myself saying the reverse when I stated that form will match content — will insist on being appropriate to it, or the other way round — and that it's in paying attention to what form requires — in consciously pursuing it, the match, the appropriateness (but also letting it be, letting it find its level) that 'content' — the next bit of plot, what to do with Arthur now he's been expelled from paradise, now he's back on the red road — will be found? If I were to give a tip it would indeed be this: everything depends upon finding a balance between control (using all your critical faculties, paying maximum attention) and letting go. Only one's inner sense (call it of form, or life, or the beat of a book) will tell whether there is grace in one's tightrope-walking act.

As I was thinking about all this, chance and a free afternoon got me into the Turner wing of the Tate. I had never before visited it. I was delighted by the room that was a monument to Turner on Perspective, and bought Maurice Davies's book on the subject. Now here was an artist (Turner) who spent years thinking he could give guidance on perspective through lectures and drawings. Who worked very hard at those lectures. And here was I arguing there was no guidance, but that of a vague kind, to be had in a comparable artistic field? Come come. . . .

What first caught my eye was Turner saying that to create an effect of grandeur with a landscape you had to place the horizon low. How true, I thought, and how it applies to literature. Stendhal creates an effect of grandeur with his battle of Waterloo at the beginning of *The Charterhouse of Parma* precisely because his vantage point is so tightly rooted in his naïve, fiery young protagonist, Fabrice. When Fabrice gets bespattered with ploughed earth by riders galloping away after they have unceremoniously stolen his horse, you get a sense of breathtaking actuality, the chaos and improvisation and brutality of battle, space, activity, scope. It isn't the apparent scope of a subject that creates real scope. Place the horizon low, yes. Use the apparently small, the individual, to get at the collective, the historical. The poets who, like the French Francis Ponge and Hélène Cixous, write about pebbles and oranges may say larger things than the poet who writes about the nuclear holocaust. It's all a question of how; but also of how astutely you've placed your horizon. Human beings are almost half-way between the infinitely small and the infinitely large. Physicists say there is more distance between the infinitely small of the Big Bang and an orange than between an orange and the expanded universe. A novel that deals with the stock exchange, or international relations and war, is not by virtue of its subject 'bigger' than one about becoming a beetle (e.g. Kafka's *Metamorphosis*) or encountering a cockroach (Lispector's *The Passion according to G.H.*). It's all a question of how — indeed, for me the low horizon is more likely to be conducive to an effect of grandeur.

I don't know about grandeur, but reflecting on what I did I suddenly realized that the feet were important — Arthur's boots. Their encounter with, their knowledge of, the road. He is, in a comic sort of way, at one point healed by a pair of silk white socks Tabby's stuffed into his pocket. Fetishism, sure. (And what does that mean?) But you can hardly go lower for your horizon.

Expounding on perspective, Turner takes an interesting distance from the classical idea, illustrated by Dürer's famed window, that there was a mathematically precise system of perspective that was capable of representing objects with complete geometrical accuracy. The system implied that the artist remained motionless, fixed at a single spot, viewing the scene with one eye only. It was explained that light rays travelled to the artist's eye from the object, forming a cone. The picture then was simply a framed intersection of this cone. Standard perspective produced depictions that appeared absolutely accurate when viewed by the spectator from the correct viewpoint. Pointing out the distortions and complexities that certain angles brought about, and how previous painters have incorporated them, Turner spoke of a 'joint coincidence' between rules and nature: 'Rules are the means, nature the end'. One could pick up on this and say that, in terms of the art of language, formal demands are the means, an insightful effect of reality the end. 'Joint coincidence' is certainly to be sought.

Hem. What formal demands? An effect of reality rather than truthfulness to 'nature', for instance the human heart? Isn't the effect of reality part and parcel of the language, its rhythm etc.? What a mess to have wandered into!

Perhaps not. And perhaps this is not as much of a digression as it might appear. That the *motionless one* eye of the observer should have been thought of as the privileged, indeed the truthful focus; that geometric rays should have been thought to be travelling between self and landscape, asserting the unity of human eye/mind and perceptible nature; that the human body itself, through geometrical cross-sections, should have been perceived as continuous with basic geometric shapes (the pyramid, the triangle, etc.), all bespeak a microcosm/macrocosm view of reality in which rational order prevails. That order, incidentally or not, tends to be male-centred, since the female is infrequently the originator of perspective, and generally one of its objects.

One of the fascinating things that Turner does is include columns, steps, pieces of ground, clothes, as a framing device for his expanded, often multi-focus perspectives. They appear so close that you feel as if you could take one step, and you'd be inside the picture. The body becomes included, not as something that is amenable to geometric perspective itself, but as part of the thing that sees, part of the seeing.

That, of course, is only part of the story. Part of the beginning of Turner.

It was no accident that he was doing this in the midst of the Romantic period, at a time when the supposedly unified and coherent subject splits for good. It was Schiller I believe who said that 'to create the subject of the creator' had now become the object of creation, or words to that effect. One hundred and eighty years on; Impressionism Cubism Surrealism Modernism Post-Modernism and a lot more in-between: it may seem impossibly remote to refer to Turner. The subject of the creator, and of his creation, protagonist and character and all, have been dissolved in so many caustic baths that there is hardly a fragment of bone left, or so you might think. There has been formal experimentation of such diversity, such a mechanization and rationalization and totalization of our darkest selves as well as discovery of our subconscious. Male protagonists, whether of poetry or prose, have been so drawn and quartered, guessed at à la James, hollowed à la Conrad and drowned à la Eliot, Finnegans-Waked and reduced to the perception of the geometry of a banana-plantation à la Robbe-Grillet; while female protagonists, this century especially, have been in turns so stream-of-consciousnessed, so Orlandoed and Bildungsromaned, defeminized and deloused and deconstructed, re-roled and made to fly alternatively or all at once, that. . . . Did I say that I could think up of some rules, some guidance to the apprentice writer?

Tips. That's more like it.

Is it?

It is all very well to take a historical view of literature and art, to relativize it, to say: this — perspective — is bound up with Western culture, a moment of white, male, imperialism. The primacy of optics, geometrical anthropomorphism, as well as those twin pillars of classical realism, character and plot, are charged with social, political, racial, gender assumptions — as, among others, feminist theory has brilliantly pointed out in the past twenty years. The fact remains that when one reads, (or looks) when one writes (or presumably, paints), the relation to life, the life of the self, the larger life, remains also immediate — whatever the parameters, the mediations. A line by Racine's Phèdre, or the accepted, white bleakness of the baby's exposure and separation in Piero della Francesca's *Nativity*, can, to me, express states I feel with absolute profundity. I am staggered that the artist should have known what he knew. There is no better form for my feeling. The appropriateness and beauty of that form provide the only relief I can find. Furthermore, enterprises like revisioning, which we connect with Modernism or Feminism, are as old as literature, as painting. Turner took on Dürer, Claude, Raphael. Racine Euripides, Shakespeare Italian chronicles, Plutarch, fairy tales, travellers' stories. Even Homer took on oral legends and histories. Colette was an astute admirer of Balzac, and Rimbaud's first efforts imitate Hugo and Baudelaire. When I take on Rimbaud and Colette, I am in substantial company.

But my exploration of gender and desire owes a lot to the revisioning of the last twenty or thirty years by women writers — Jean Rhys's *Wide Sargasso Sea*, Christa Wolf's *Cassandra*, Angela Carter's *The Bloody Chamber*. . . . It has to do with wanting to alter expectations, habits — with gaining leeway — freedom, and through freedom, hope. What distinguishes these revisionings is the awareness that there is no room for me, a human being, in that script, and the desire to make room for me, and the likes of me. This entails re-reading that other script, feeling that because it is strong, because it is so powerfully human (like *Jane Eyre*) there will be gaps, repressions, unrecognized moments, and these will be my points of entry. *Wide Sargasso Sea* gives Mrs Rochester, alias Bertha Mason, the room, the human fullness her initial author had denied her. Women writers have needed, and still need, to revision the mythic scripts of the past. Often openly, or by implication, they universalize or essentialize debasing and sometimes downright dehumanizing versions of woman-hood. When Charlotte Brontë depicted Mrs Rochester as mad, colonial, bestial, subhuman in every way, she was settling bitter accounts with the professor's wife, her rival. She was using every trick in the nationalistic, orientalizing and religious book to do her down, destroy her as Jane's rival. Yet as she did so, something of the fierce passion in her found expression through Mrs Rochester's eerie doublings of Jane: it is when Jane is at her most rebellious that she hears the madwoman's laugh. It is by challenging and totally rewriting the nationalism and colonialism, the vindictive sense of evangelical propriety and sanity of *Jane Eyre* that Jean Rhys, through her protagonist Antoinette, finds her way not only to lyrical expression of her own Caribbean childhood and suppressed selfhood, but to a strand in Charlotte Brontë's text that had remained until then dormant. Revisioning can be an emancipation both for the writer and the revised author's text.

It can also be gaining access to enlarged possibilities. Because of their beauty and power, and the depth of experience and the intensity of work that has gone into them, of their enduring appeal, there is much human truth in mythic scripts. They are powerfully influential, self-generating. If what I want to say is truthful, it needs to find its place in the real sun — where those scripts are (however blinkered or partisan in part they may be). If I want to make a difference, make room for whatever humanity there is in me that these scripts deny, I must wrestle with them. Sneak into them, smell them, touch them, listen to them, let them inhabit me. From the intercourse, the cohabitation, something that will include and express me, and the likes of me, may be born.

One may be surprised by what happens. I was trying to reinvent a man, Rimbaud, who was deeply misogynistic. There is vitriol in poems like 'Mes Petites amoureuses'. Real vitriol. He throws it at women's bodies, souls. How does one stop anger and fear from turning into such poison? How does one, being a woman, reinventing the voice of a woman-hater, save oneself from self-hatred?

Is one trying to come to terms with one's self-hatred?

Turner's attention to perspective and his developing sense of its inadequacies, his feeling that it was 'the gossamer down — a web too weak to hold . . . the forms of muscular exertion [and] unable to assume the flowing undulating forms of female beauty', his twisting and turning, his growing passion with curves, and more and more the whirls and mists and Impressionistic wanderings from line, may all bespeak a nineteenth-century struggle, particular gender attitudes. The fact remains that when I begin to write a character like Arthur, what he sees, where he sees it from, how inner state merges with and colours outer state (i.e. a certain, inevitable form of anthropomorphism) all come into play. For surely one writes in order to make sense of the world, find a form that will hold it and us? For me the immediacy of touch and drives, in my Arthur, is rather like those steps and balustrades and bits of grass close to the frames in Turner's paintings, that make you feel you can step in. The more he goes, the more he — you — need it. Even the vortices are framed in squares. The squares hold it. Rimbaud had begun with alexandrines. The old beat, the beat that so fits the French language, later perhaps held him, enabled him to hold the white-heat prose of *The Illuminations*.

The resilient, enduring need for stories, plots, incidents, characters, is the reliability, the aesthetic reassurance and pleasure that they provide. Perhaps they are a bit like perspective and subject to someone like Turner. 'We only see the world through two holes in our head,' Spinoza said. Theoreticians of perspective had tried to make it one hole. Was it because he had strained so long to combine that ideal hold with the many holes in the human body, his human body — ears, nostrils, pores and the cock's one eye, the cock's blind or seeing eye? — that Turner painted his *Ulysses and Polyphemus*, the blinded hole searching the mists and swirls for the misty swirling wounding ship? What appalling knowledge of pain got the man to paint the plight of the Roman who failed to bring back the Roman prisoners from Carthage, whose eyelids were cut off and who was exposed to the scorching sun? And all the vortices, light, water, air, of the later paintings? Would they have held, would he have been able to arrive at those depths, those forms, if he had not fought that first struggle with structure — with perspective?

The converse is true. If he had not travelled so deep, so far, into self-knowledge and through pain, all the apprenticeship, the craft, the rules, the angles, would have been for nothing. Shirking the worst — avoiding extremities — will not avail. Artists are those who have no choice. Or leave themselves none.

Anthropomorphism. At one time it looked to me as if we had left that behind. Part of the arrogance of Western culture:

geometry and privileged viewpoints expressive of power relations, economic, social, racial, gender hierarchies with a dominant male subject at the top, or behind the lenses. Those privileged positions anyway had been shaken by the discovery of the subconscious, by Relativism, and were no longer tenable, though, of course, they went on perpetuating their power games.

Now I am not so sure. It is crucial for anyone who believes in humans' equal right to being human not to go on building meanings — vantage-points — over somebody else. Or at the expense of — let's say nature (a term like 'environment' in itself implying a privileged vantage-point, and 'creation' a religious viewpoint). But for me the idea of finding a relation between self and world has come back to the top of the agenda. That implies imaginatively becoming at home in the world. Is this anthropomorphism? Yes and no. For one thing that our awareness of the subconscious has done is to show us how much the outside world, and the nether world, and others — parental figures, families, plus a whole menagerie of beasts and vices (as Baudelaire said) — are in us. And yes, of course Baudelaire and Racine and Dante and Breughel and Turner knew this. They had different ways of knowing it. But when we read them, look at their works, we keep seeing what we are. Revisioning in that sense is saying what we are, where we are, how we are: our way.

Four

Arthur was back on the red road. What was going to get him from there, after his grief at having lost Tabby and the shelter of her attic, to a point at which he could meet up with her again, on other terms?

I can now see that when I first wrote the second half of my tale, I was shirking the issue. I thought a darker version of fantasy would do. I was looking for escape. I thought that the detour Arthur had made would have changed his attitude to the rest of his life. He would say no to destruction.

He got to a deserted village, the empty inn. In the mirror above the counter, he re-lived his childhood. He walked to the church across the square. Sitting in the confessional was a 'prêtre souillon' (Baudelaire's dirty priest, and an off-shoot of *Un Coeur sous une soutane*). The priest had the manner of Verlaine. He was married. Mounting a solitary and anguished vigil at the presbytery window was a young woman dressed in crisp linen, very much like Verlaine's wife Mathilde. Catching sight of her, Arthur hates her. She is respectable domestic Woman, the enemy. There is a silent battle of wills between them. Arthur goes to the confessional. He speaks into the priest's ear. He seduces the priest. Which is what the priest has been longing for.

But at the last minute Arthur says no.

His refusal releases them both.

Like Mallarmé's faun, like Hugo's Satyr, like all the other Orpheuses, in disappointed yearning the priest sings. He sings the *Romance sans paroles, Jadis et naguère*. His singing is so airy, so beautiful that the village comes to life. Arthur is freed from the red road. He finds his way to the sea.

La Route rouge slumbered for a few years in its green-and-black parchment-covered notebook.

I must have mentioned it to somebody or other, because out of the blue (the sea at Plymouth) I was asked to go and give a reading from it, in English of course, at a Rimbaud centenary celebration. Rimbaud had died in 1892.

It was a lovely day, that celebration, a sharing of the poetry. Everyone there loved Rimbaud, his translator Oliver Bernard, the host Bernard Samuels, poets. At the end of my reading a man said, 'have you ever thought that the red road might have to do with female menstruation?'. I had not: to me the red road had to do with the two Franco-Prussian wars, especially the 1914 war. Trench warfare, the earth drinking the blood, eating the bodies of millions of men in the flat northern plains. My other novella — my Herodiade — had also been about that.

The man who asked that question turned out to be poet Peter Redgrove, the co-author with Penelope Shuttle of *The Wise Wound*.

What he said was a gift. A revelation.

I went and read *The Wise Wound*.

Valéry tells how he was stuck over 'Le cimetière marin'. He evokes a gang of workers straining to heave the Parthenon columns into place. The columns were such a weight that the taut ropes began to fray. If they broke the columns would crash, smash to fragments, crushing the men underneath. Suddenly from the crowd a voice was heard: 'Mouillez les cordes'. Wet the ropes.

Peter Redgrove's suggestion to me was 'Wet the ropes'.

I was stuck over Part II for five years. Five years in which I stayed in the empty inn, poured seductive words into the dirty priest's ear. Five years in which I alternately hated and pitied Mathilde, made her win, then robbed her of her all.

Five years in which to imagine how the hell a man who hates women, hates the mother, hates home so much, who cannot even stomach the rather subverted and debauched version of home he'd established with the 'foolish virgin', his fellow-poet, could ever be free from longing and revulsion. The wind-soled vagabond, the real Rimbaud, spent the rest of his life fleeing. Nowhere to go: he'd imagined it all, done it all. Gone twice full circle already. Once in 'The Drunken Boat', sick of all seas and longing for the black childhood puddle. Another time in *A Season in Hell*, left at the end of a bold voyage into the underworld 'rendu à la terre, avec la réalité rugueuse à étreindre', 'restored to the earth, with nothing but rough reality to embrace'.

As the novella stirred and took life again, I became aware of the cost it demanded. I had saved up on pain. I had thought dreams and visions would do, that they could be got at easily. I had not realized there was a price to pay. I thought some lives could avoid hell, and that my Arthur might be one of the lucky ones. I didn't know that you can't get free from hell unless you have been there, and know you have been there.

The magnitude of Rimbaud's despair, of his violence, hit me. There was no way of even minimally touching that without going inside, finding out what violence I could actually imagine. I was appalled by Arthur's sadism. By the intensity of Paul's masochism. In 'real life' Verlaine's masochism, it seems, was the obverse side of sadism: in later years, in an alcoholic delirium, he turned on his widowed mother, brought crashing down the glass jars in which she'd kept the 'pickled foetuses' (as Pound calls them) of her miscarried children. . . .

(Arthur is kneeling in the confessional where Paul sits. Arthur imagines their future).

> I knew him. I hated him, the pitted flesh, the greasy cassock. Married, was he? Defrocked, is what they're called. If ever a frock suited a slut it fitted those limp balls, that pate as bare as baby's buttocks. I keened for him. The man's exquisite grace. He knew about the songs of the turtle-doves drowning in their river shadows, and how the slender water-jets vanish amid the tall fronds.
>
> I wanted tattooing all over. Ships' masts, eagles' talons, to ripple and fan out as I moved. I would be all ink. War ink. The outer skin wasn't enough: I would tattoo my heart. Not a pore of my mother's son's flesh left. I would be ink all over. Self-written. At the head of marching armies.
>
> I wouldn't have defended Paris against the Prussians or the Versaillais. Not me. No ramparts for me, no Père Lachaise walls to line me up against and then shoot me with the other Communards. I would have besieged Versailles. And stormed it. Not a shred of silk, not a block of marble left. No quarters given. I would have massacred every one of those soldiers, in their prim red and blue. I plunged my bayonet into their guts. And again. They begged. I knew no mercy. I would hang their scalps round my belt. My shit and piss streaked with their blood.
>
> I knew everything about him.
>
> The taste of his sweat. The acrid weakness bathing him, softening his flesh. He smelt of maceration. Chrysanthemum stems long rotten in a vase. I knew his fear, when the Republican guard came for him to fight for the Commune, while just imagining gunpowder and ramparts, the Versaillais

in their clean uniforms cocking their guns, the long points of the bayonets, how easily they would . . . he dirtied himself. He hid under the bed. He told wifey to hide his gun in the cupboard, under the piles of sheets which, unlike him, smelt of lavender. He was the place for refuse!

I loved him for his abjection. His limp flesh, open to all, all the liquids. His pores were spongy. I saw the grain of his skin under the beard, the hanging ear lobe. Over-soft man, I cherish your weakness. Anything can get in there. Settle in.

I cannot forgive him: he sought me, *me*! for a father and a mother.

I hate him for having adored in me a male I hate.

How he clung!

(Arthur imagines their progress. They're in London, tramping, staying in a Newchapel flat. They've gone on one of their inimitable pub crawls. They're rowing. Arthur beats Paul up.)

He was on the floor. I plucked at his beard. He squealed and squirmed. My fingers groped, met the smooth, the sickening baldness. Baby baldness. Slipped to his sparse, longish hair. It came out in tufts in my hands. He was bigger than me. My boots were on his shins. Holding down his limp flesh. He let me beat him up.

I loathed the ecstasy on his face.

I wanted to wind my fingers in his long blond hair. His tawny hair. I wanted hair that fell to his ankles. I wanted to throw myself on the drowning body of Ophelia. She was floating among the reeds. Her clothes had buoyed her up. She was singing and I jumped on her. She was all water-logged ballooning linen and I closed her mouth with mine and choked her song and my weight pushed her under water and we were all sandy saltless sweet water. She began to struggle and I tore at those floating weedy clothes and she wrapped her legs around me and my tongue sank into her mouth and hers came alive and filled my palate and we were full of each other straining right out like fledgling birds, like cactus flowers when the pistils stretch out from the depths of the green throat. Her eyes opened under water and they were green like Tabby's and we swung upright and rose to the surface and became unstuck and there we were gasping, all dripping and spittle, and light and laughter and arms round each other's shoulders we swam to the shore with both outer arms.

We'd see to the imbecile, Hamlet, later.
We'd let them see to each other, Laertes and Claudius and
Hamlet and the grave-diggers. The lot.
His nose was bleeding.
I licked the blood on his lips.
I couldn't stand the bliss on his face.

Next day I fled.

The Wise Wound links all sorts of speculations that question
and reverse familiar Freudian patterns. Period pain, societal
and psychological disfunction, the loss of rhythm, of
attunement to natural rhythms, are seen as the effects or
symptoms of a fear and repression of the female body, the
natural ebb and flow of creative blood. What if, as Faegerman
believes (quoted in *The Wise Wound*), castration were 'the
bloody bridge that leads from masculinity to feminity', and
what if men suffering from profound disturbances, ranging
from depression to schizophrenic hallucination were producing a knowledge, and fear of, menstrual rhythms that erupts
after a long repression? For Bettelheim, 'menstruation can be
seen as the gate of blood that leads back to childhood, that is
to the time when we were not psychologically *neuter* as
infants, but *deuter*, that is comprising the undeveloped qualities of both sexes, like a complete being "trailing clouds of
glory", like Plato's bisexual being whom god split into male
and female.'
    Sexual roles, Shuttle and Redgrove argue, are given at
puberty. The 'other' goes underground, but is not eradicated:
'it is possible that this gate of blood opens every month in the
woman's menstruation'. If valued, ways to deal with the
damage of childhood might be found. 'For the man, the gate
to past time and therefore to his feminine side, either does not
open at all, or it is given a chance to open by acquiring a
'symbolic wound' at his puberty initiation.' Hence initiation
rites, as interpreted by Bettelheim (Shuttle and Redgrove,
pp 72–3).
    I had not thought of the red road as connected with castra-
tion, even though the fear of being devoured, the eat-or-be-

eaten, was such a powerful motif. The green grass, all
mouths. . . . Even less had I thought of menstruation. Yet
why did I have no men in my earthly paradise domain? Why
was it the mother and daughter/mother who threatened Arthur
and chased him away? Shuttle and Redgrove re-interpret a
famous childhood dream by Jung: having descended down a
stone stairway and through a round arch closed by a green
curtain, the child sees a huge trunk-like flesh thing with a
round, one-eyed head, sat on a red cushion on a throne to
which a red carpet leads. His mother's voice says 'this is the
man-eater'. Jung realized years later that this was 'a ritual
phallus', and that the dream was alerting him to 'the motif of
cannibalism that underlies the symbolism of the mass'. What
if the dream were of entering a womb-place, with the cervix
with its round head seated on blood; and the dream expressing
the child's fear of his own sexual excitation and of the womb
or mother as 'man-eater'? (Shuttle and Redgrove, pp 106–7).

What would such an interpretation make of Turner's *Ulysses
and Polyphemus*? 'Deuter'. . . .

It tallied with my red and green, with the cannibalistic
motif, Arthur's fear of women.

It did not tell me how to get him from fear to acceptance.

But the ropes now were wet.

Five

This is some of the stories of one story.
There are many others.
Reasons why we write.

Michèle Roberts

Post-Script

The semi-transparent envelope: it's hard to see the writing inside; a bill? torn-up fragments of letters? When you write a novel you have to make out the form. Discover it. Find it. (Latin *invenio*: I find, I come upon, and so I invent.) You find the form by meditating on the demands of the subject-matter.

Inspiration: something arrives, swims up, a message in a bottle bobs tantalizingly and you peer at it, not quite able to make it out. That pearly paper of the window in the envelope; that rippled glass of the floating bottle. You have to destroy something, paper or glass, to get at what's inside. Lovely aggressive destruction, like when I was a child making mud dishes and smashing the porcelain head of an antique doll.

I begin with a haunting, an obsession. Something's nagging at me, bothering me. A visual image appears, or a bit of one. I translate it into words. *A vision of a red virgin in the woods*: from this, like silk spun from a cocoon, eventually came the whole of my sixth novel. I write novels to understand the wordless images, spin a story around them that will lay them, like ghosts. Also to answer questions: can mothers truly love daughters? Does a woman belong in this world and is she allowed to have a house of her own? (I realized only recently that all my novels feature homeless women, that novels are the paper houses I build, then inhabit.)

At the same time I write novels to explore the form, to find out just what it can do. Different each time. The content (those images, those nagging questions) shapes the form; only that form can demonstrate that content. Yes, form *is* content. The story of a woman obsessed with material possessions *had* to be told as her inventory of the contents of her house; the story of the cousin she quarrelled with *had* to be a saint's autobiography that could quarrel with the version contained in the inventory. Clash of points of view; clash of forms. I want to write in a way that relishes language, its materiality like paint. The language is what matters. It has, is, body.

I might spend from six months to a year, these days, struggling to discover the form the novel could take, before I discover it. Struggle can mean just sitting quietly attending to all the problems, naming them, listening to them. Jim, who's a painter, always says to me: make the problem part of the subject. You do that at the level of content, also of form. So during this period, when the imagination needs to be fed and stimulated, I read voraciously (literary theory when it comes under my nose, thrillers, Edwardian guidebooks filched from my aunt's house, books which arrive randomly as gifts or cast-offs), I record my dreams (the novel always starts here), I scribble madly in chaotic notebooks, I make lots of false starts, I make notes, I doodle.

There's nothing I like better than this hermit's life of writing, solitude all day and every day, seven days a week if I so choose. Even when the writing is going badly or not at all (silence and writer's block are normal, inextricably part of the writing process, you learn to trust in absence and inability and powerlessness and the need to wait quietly and patiently) this is where I want to be: in my study, on my own, all day long. (At night, when the working day is done, I want all the pleasures of conviviality; conversation and wine and food and sex.) Until I was twenty or so I thought I had a religious vocation, wanted to become a Carmelite, spend my life in prayer, in silence. It strikes me, looking at what I've written here, that writing is a bit like waiting on God (also like Keats' negative capability): trusting in the darkness, opening yourself up to what comes, being empty. Making actually feels very active to me. Perhaps prayer can be too. I think I've invented my own version of the convent, becoming a writer: no Mother Superior needed; lots of good food as muse (see below); an image of God changing from a distant, absent, invisible and frightening authority figure of either sex (sometimes — I mean I have many images of God) to that of a close, warm, present and nourishing body, which first I've imaged as female and maternal but now also find in the body of the man I love and desire. Writing's a bisexual practice: you have to be both active and passive; 'masculine' and 'feminine' need to be in relation; the mother relates to the child inside the self; all this is an ever-changing dance, never static.

I want to put in a word on food and its relationship to writing, because it matters to me. Writing is a physical act. I don't use a word-processor (I always want to call it a food-processor) but a tiny ancient portable typewriter with very bouncy keys you can hit satisfyingly hard, and with smudgy ink ribbons. I like scribbling in pen over typed drafts; I like the act of the hand moving, the traces of ink, the sound of the nib *scritch scritch scritch*; the palimpsests I produce, memory encoded on the page; the history of three drafts, perhaps, visible on a single sheet. That's all very physical, close to drawing (I wanted to be a painter as well as a nun, was devastated when I failed art 'O' level with grade Z). Writing feels like pulling something out of my insides; I've made it inside, now must draw it out, put it out. It's painful or pleasurable, depending on how the work's going, but it diminishes and empties me, I've lost part of myself, I become hungry. Meals are fuel and reward. At these times I want hearty delicious dishes; lots of pasta, garlic, olive oil; bread. I also find that cooking myself a quick but delicious lunch, to be eaten at the typewriter, will get me through my writer's block of the morning and produce pages of writing. I eat with one hand and type with the other. The mother in me feeds the baby in me.

Mother and baby cooperate to produce the writing. The baby is the artist but is helped by the mother. I think I began writing because of a profound sense of lack of a maternal figure, of the absence of that internal image, of desperate need and terror at abandonment. Writing, I open up to those feelings; very painful, very frightening. Eating a good lunch as part of the working day soothes that desperate baby, nurtures her. I've worked all this out since stopping smoking two and a half years ago: I had to face my mad lust for five lunches a day while writing, and do something about it! The answer was not abstinence and self-denial, but permissiveness. I do get plumper while writing novels, I've discovered now; I'm not totally comfortable about it because part of me thinks I should be slim, but I'm living with it. Perhaps I'm becoming less perfectionist, more able to tolerate the feelings of rage and sorrow and loss of control/self/ego that burst up when I write and which can seem like incipient madness; the unconscious breaking through; sometimes disturbing and scary, sometimes bringing tears and joy. It's an emotional business!

So there's cooking, and there's taking little naps whenever needed (like a semi-colon in the day; a chance to dream up the next image I need; or, let's be honest, just to sleep off lunch. But I can't work seven hours without a siesta and always take one), and then there's housekeeping. For me, writing is a way of keeping house; building myself the house I felt, deep inside, I wasn't allowed to have because I was a kind of monster raging with forbidden desires and feelings, tearing it down and re-building it. So I've never been much of a housewife because it wasn't included in my self-image; yet on the other hand, I've always loved decorating and furnishing and arranging, on a shoe-string, the many places I've lived in. Now, in my forties, for the first time feeling *at home*, living with Jim, I'm still useless at dusting and sweeping, just as he is, but I'm happy to spend time cleaning the kitchen, where I do my precious cooking, and washing my carefully collected bits of French china that we eat off, and endlessly re-hanging the pictures and watering the plants and laundering the lace tablecloth and lighting all the candles. This is all sensual to me, I do it on my own terms and in my own time, and visiting friends are amazed by how pretty, and dusty, the flat is.

What I'm trying to say is: sweeping the kitchen floor, putting away the saucepans, acts as a helpful image to me of rootling about in my imagination and re-ordering the images there, sorting things out. In this sense housework is not oppressive. Of course, it would be if I felt economically dependent on a bossy husband ordering/expecting me to do it. Jim, being an artist, laughs at it. I like living in chaos, in these rooms we're always changing, in this rather tumbledown house that we're never finished repairing and decorating. I like flux, change. I'm about to buy a little house in France (my maternal country in which I speak my mother's tongue) and that, I know, because I shall own it and it will be *mine*, I will dust and paint and polish to an inch of its life. Because it represents the maternal body; the body of love; once lost and damaged; now found again, made reparation to. That's the house in which I hope to write my next novel, in which I shall dust, polish and paint words, endlessly re-draft them, be as completely obsessive as I need to be about getting it right, writing as well as I can. Really, I think, there's this great hope in me to write better next time, to improve.

Thank you very much, Nicole, Susan, Sue, for letting me join in this conversation of yours.